IN CONSIDERATION OF THE READER'S TIME
THIS SHORT BOOK WAS CREATED...

QUICK NOTES FOR
THE PROPHET

REVEALING THE MAN OF LAWLESSNESS

Ronald B. Stetton

In consideration of the reader's time this short book was created...

<u>*Quick Notes*</u>

for

The Prophet

The intention of this booklet is to give the reader an opportunity to quickly review the material and then decide whether it is worth one's time to read the book, review all references, and consider the evidence revealing
The Prophet

IN CONSIDERATION OF THE READER'S TIME
THIS SHORT BOOK WAS CREATED...

QUICK NOTES FOR
THE PROPHET

REVEALING THE MAN OF LAWLESSNESS

RONALD B. STETTON

Quick Notes For The Prophet by Ronald B. Stetton
Copyright © 2023 by Ronald B. Stetton
All Rights Reserved.
ISBN: 978-1-59755-579-1

Published by: ADVANTAGE BOOKS™   www.advbookstore.com

This book and parts thereof may not be reproduced in any form, stored in a retrieval system or transmitted in any form by any means (electronic, mechanical, photocopy, recording or otherwise) without prior written permission of the author, except as provided by United States of America copyright law.

Scripture taken from the HOLY BIBLE, NEW INTERNATIONAL VERSION NIV. Copyright 1973, 1978, 1984 by International Bible Society. Used by permission of Zondervan Publishing House

KJV Reference Bible. Introductions and Outlines to the Books of the Bible Copyright 1977; KJV Concordance Copyright 1992, 1994 by the Zondervan Corporation

The Strongest Strong's Exhaustive Concordance of the Bible Copyright 2001 by Zondervan

More Than A Carpenter, Copyright 1977 by Josh McDowell

The Holy Qur'an with English Translation and Commentary 2002, Ahmadiyya Anjuman Isha'at Islam Lahore Inc., U.S.A.

A Manual of Hadith; Ahmadiyya Anjuman Ishaat Islam Lahore USA Inc.

Library of Congress Catalog Number: 2023931407

Names:	Stetton, Ronanld B., Author
Title:	*Quick Notes For The Prophet*
	Ronald B. Stetton
	Advantage Books, 2023
Identifiers:	ISBN (print): 9781597555791
Subjects:	Christian Life: Inspirational

First Printing March 2023
23 24 25 26 27 28   10 9 8 7 6 5 4 3 2 1

Foreword

What Does This Material Hope to Accomplish?

For centuries, men have been pondering the writings of Moses and the prophets who followed him. His Spiritually guided pen has been complemented by the likes of Isaiah, Jeremiah, Daniel, Matthew, Mark, Luke, John, Paul, and many others. These men and their prophetic insight have given us the story of man in written form – from beginning to end. In total, their lives and prophetic writings spanned nearly 1,400 years. As foretold, much of the world mocks and laughs at those who believe in the written testimonies of God's trustworthy servants. That collective mockery is soon to subside.

Though proof of God's existence was personally delivered by Jesus and reiterated in written form, the historical aspect has yet to be compiled and presented in a comparative manner such as this. In an ironic twist, further proof of God comes about by revealing the identity of a diabolical character, The Prophet, that history knows too well. Many of God's true prophets describe this man of mystery and they do so in the grandest of fashions. Their vivid imagery and unique visions have provided mankind with an array of details surrounding The Prophet and his evil plan. They have given us insight about the things he would say, the things he would do, the things he would accomplish, and the wicked role of opposition he was certain to fulfill. The world has come to know such a man. Until now he has flown under the radar and, without being recognized, he continues with his rebellious acts. He has hidden himself under a veil of contemptuous deceit and hides in plain sight as *The Prophet of God*.

This book assists the reader in understanding that…

- Lucifer was a man
- The false prophet was a man
- The false prophet was a fallen, tormented man
- The little horn, described by Daniel, was a man
- He began his rise to power during the fall of the Roman Empire
- He was a religious king who exalted himself above Jesus and the prophets

- He is the root of the abomination that causes desolation upon the Temple Mount
- He was the first man to speak the seven thunders
- He boastfully admits to changing the Laws of God
- His actions and words constitute the biblical definition of *antichrist*
- He repeatedly states his denial of the Father and Son as God
- His spoken word leads the world away from the Father, His Son, and the Spirit
- His woeful lessons endorsing theft, murder, and destruction attest to his lawlessness
- His departure from previous Scripture includes the introduction of a foreign god
- His verbal presentation of 'revelations' make him the speaking image of his god
- He affirms that being 'the foremost to serve,' he would be the metaphorical son
- He personally victimized the residents and travelers within Sheba and Dedan
- He boasts of plundering and looting merchants of the Tarshish
- He has convinced many that his role as a thief is honorary
- His people have been taught that he is 'the perfect model' for men
- He introduced himself as *the bright morning star*
- His stern instruction and lethal lessons lack any hint of grace
- He has succeeded in utilizing terror as a weapon of righteousness
- His instruction encourages the utilization of murder, crucifixion, and beheading
- His instruction of opposition encourages amputations and imprisonment
- His battlefield code phrase of "Peace and security!" has become his nation's greeting
- His existence, recorded word, and historical accomplishments are a matter of record
- His recorded testimony serves as further proof that the biblical God is 'God'

TABLE OF CONTENTS

Foreword 5
What Does This Material Hope to Accomplish? 5
Preface 9
Chapter 1: Lucifer Was a Man 11
Chapter 2: Little Horn with a Boastful Mouth 15
    Daniel's descriptive warning of the false prophet (7:2-25) 15
    Stern-Faced Destruction 16
    Daniel's descriptive warning of the Stern man (8:23-25) 16
Chapter 3: After The Tax Collector 23
    Daniel's warning of the man's appearance (11:20-33) 23
Chapter 4: Religious King Who Exalted Himself 27
Chapter 5: Seeing The Abomination That Causes Desolation 31
    Unveiling the warnings of Daniel 9 & Matthew 24 31
Chapter 6: Sound of Seven Thunders 33
    John's warning about the seven "oft-repeated" verses (Revelation 10) ... 33
Chapter 7: Revelation Before the Day Of The Lord 35
    Paul's warning about the man of lawlessness (2 Thessalonians 2) ... 35
Chapter 8: Antichrist Prophet 37
    John's definitive warning about the Antichrist (1 John 2) 37
Chapter 9: The Speaking Image 39
    John's description of the false prophet (Revelation 13) 39
Chapter 10: Shorts
    Victimizing Sheba & Dedan 41
    Body Of Believers 41
    Thief 42
    Fallen 43

Jerusalem Unmatched	43
Succeeding In Terror	44
Our World Led Astray	45
Plague of Frogs	46
Beheaded Because of Testimony	48
Peace and Safety	48

Chapter 11: The Odds 51
    A NUMERIC DEMONSTRATION ABOUT THE ONE MAN WHO HAS FULFILLED THIS VILLAINOUS ROLE ... 51

Chapter 12: The Whole World Waits 53
    WE HAVE ARRIVED 53

Preface

The Prophet reintroduces a man that most people thought they already knew. His is a household name. In one way or another, he has affected the lives of nearly everyone who has lived and breathed on earth in the last 14 centuries. His life and its impact on our world can be nothing less than prophetic. His actions and words are among those that most Bible enthusiasts should easily recognize. Yet, his intrigue has succeeded and gone undetected for centuries.

As the reader progresses through this book, he or she will likely become overwhelmed by a sense of repetition. In most books, repetitious dialogue can lead to boredom. Boredom can lead to a loss of interest. And a loss of interest usually ends with a premature dismissal of the subject. But dismissal is not likely in this case. One of the most amazing mysteries of the Bible is how so many of God's servants could write about the same man as a beast, a horn, an exalted king, a demon, a number, and a prophet while their wild imagery and perfect detail depicts the man who would directly oppose Christ. Each prophetic warning has key-word descriptions of this man's verbal lessons and historical accounts. It is the sum of these pieces that paints a picture of the biblical villain and the terrifying kingdom he has built.

The repetition is intentional – as is the broad scope of imagery that the prophets were given to make so many believe that these are all stand-alone events and not the life and times of any one, single man. Take a moment to recognize how only God could orchestrate the Word in such a manner. God tells us that he will do as He pleases. In this case, He chose to give the world all that they needed to recognize the biblical villain, but He did so in a manner that released the villain's identity at the proper time. Inspiring is God's amazing precision and the ability of His prophets to accurately describe *the Opposer*. This is God's intent. The menace is to be revealed when God decides it is time to reveal him. Time and again, the reader will hear about the life and successes of this arrogant outlaw. But, with every telling, additional bits of evidence will be added to compound the monumental case against him. Be patient. Read it through. Be among the many who are soon to recognize this mystery of God and how He was able to keep such obvious truths hidden well within the fog of man's delusions.

The book of Daniel warns that 'war will continue until the end.' One of Daniel's successors, Matthew, expands upon that warning; 'You will hear of wars and rumors of war… nation will rise against nation, and kingdom against kingdom.' The key to understanding the war is to recognize the opposing teaching between God's promised Messiah and The Prophet. Their teachings are compared below…

"…a time is coming when anyone who kills you will think he is offering a service to God. They will do such things because they have not known the Father or me. I have told you this, so that when the time comes you will remember that I warned you" – Jesus

"The only punishment of those who wage war against [god] and [me] and strive to [break our laws] is that they should be murdered…" – The Prophet

Chapter 1

Lucifer Was a Man

Isaiah's descriptive warning of Lucifer the man (14:3-23)

Lucifer…
We all know the name. It doesn't matter how we were brought up, what religion we practiced, who our fathers were or how well we were educated - the name *Lucifer* is known to us all. His name is the essence of evil. Most people believe that Lucifer is just another of Satan's many names. But that belief is easily refuted by biblical testimony. Lucifer was a man. He was the man who shook the earth and made kingdoms tremble. He was the man who made the world a desert and overthrew its cities. Lucifer was the man who would not let his captives go home. The startling reality is that the world has already been acquainted to this man. His kingdom lives, breaths, and grows as men read this.

Without knowing or understanding the warnings of Isaiah, those who worship this man could not possibly recognize the biblical significance of his statements. Without reading and understanding Isaiah's testimony about Lucifer, few would have the ability to recognize the marks or written statements made within The Prophet's own little book. Following are a few of his recorded statements and the narrated explanations of his remarks:

- "… the *Comer by night* is here [The] Prophet. [The] Prophet appeared when total darkness spread on earth. It may be added that [*the Comer by night*] is also the name given to the *morning star*."
- "I seek refuge in the Lord of *the Dawn*"
- "… When a man serves God, he may metaphorically be called a son of God, and therefore [The] Prophet, being the foremost of those to serve, would be a son in that sense…"
- "… on another night when his heart saw, and The Prophet, his eyes slept but his heart did not sleep; and such are the prophets, their eyes sleep but their hearts do not sleep, then Gabriel accompanied him and he carried him to heaven"

- "… The significance of the ascension was the spiritual eminence of [The] Prophet indicated his triumph in the world…"
- "… The Prophet does not err (sic), and would rise to the highest eminence to which man can rise."
- "… His being carried to the Temple at Jerusalem signified that he would also inherit the blessings of the Israelite prophets."
- "…[God] has no son; so I am the foremost of those who serve (God)"
- "[The Most High] is taken from the injunction to The Prophet to glorify his nourisher to perfection [god], *The Most High*, the indication clearly being that The Prophet himself would be raised to the highest position."

According to the written testimony above, the reader can easily answer the following:

- Did The Prophet consider himself to be the morning star?
    The answer would be Yes!

- Did The Prophet consider himself to be the son of the Dawn?
    The answer would be Yes!

- Did The Prophet say in his heart, "I will ascend to heaven"?
    The answer would be Yes!

- Did The Prophet say in his heart, "I will raise my throne above the stars of God"?
    The answer would be Yes!

- Did The Prophet say in his heart, "I will sit enthroned on the mount of assembly [Temple Mount]"?
    The answer would be Yes!

- Did The Prophet say in his heart, "[I will sit enthroned] on the utmost heights of the sacred mountain [God]"?
    The answer would be Yes!

- Did The Prophet say in his heart, "I will ascend above the tops of the clouds [claim ascension]"?
    The answer would be Yes!

- Did The Prophet say in his heart, "I will make myself like the Most High"?
    The answer would be Yes!

In a like manner and in accordance to documented events, the reader can find more answers to the questions:

- Did The Prophet's actions and teachings shake the earth and made kingdoms tremble"?
    The answer would be Yes!

- Did The Prophet's actions and teachings make the world a desert, overthrow its cities, and refuse to let his captives go home"?
    The answer would again be Yes!

In consideration of these things, if Lucifer was a man who had an undeniable, recorded history that would account for all these statements and descriptions – is there reason for men continue to look for another?

Ronald B. Stetton

Chapter 2

Little Horn with a Boastful Mouth

Daniel's descriptive warning of the false prophet – he who had eyes and a mouth (7:2-25)

In the 27th book of the Bible, Daniel gives the reader multiple warnings about a nefarious character who will:

- Subdue three kingdoms
- Speak out against the Father and His Son
- Oppress God's people
- Change the set times
- Change the Laws of God to laws of his foreign god

This chapter tells the reader how the man who fulfilled the promised actions of Lucifer (Isaiah 14) has also fulfilled the conditions and aspects of *the little horn* described by Daniel in chapter 7.

- He has "…subdued three kings." The nations of Sheba and Dedan fell victim to his sword and currently remain enslaved by his laws. This is the result of The Prophet's counterfeit miracles and his misleading testimony. In addition, he personally pillaged the traveling caravans who carried the wares of the merchants of the Tarshish. Thus, he subdued Sheba, Dedan and the Tarshish

- He has "… spoken out against the Most High." This is the man who introduced a foreign god. This new god was given the name of *The Most High*. The man who introduced this foreign god also testified that his 'God has no son' and that he, The Prophet, 'is the foremost to serve.' By his own testimony, he stated that he is ranked as the most high ever to live and serve God

- He has "… oppressed God's saints" for over 14 centuries. He and his Prophetiers have done everything in their power to murder, crucify, amputate, behead, or imprison anyone who caused or causes mischief in the land. Mischief is defined by him as disregarding his new and improved laws. Chief among those who have suffered under his oppressive behavior are Christians and Jews. His aggressive nature is neither incidental, nor is it a matter of coincidence. His intentional oppression continues by way of recorded directives and commands

- He has "... tried to change the set times." His efforts have largely succeeded. His followers adhere to their own calendar. Instead of recognizing Anno Domini (A.D.) as the year of our Lord, they have adopted Anno Hijra (A.H.). Anno Hijra is a period when The Prophet was driven from one city to another. This moment in time came about almost six centuries after Jesus was crucified

- He has "... changed the laws." No one can successfully argue against this. He boastfully admits that the Laws of God were outdated. The same Laws that Jesus adhered to were cast away by this man. He tossed them aside nearly five centuries after Jesus' prophets laid down their pens. It was The Prophet who changed the Laws that had been written upon Stone and cut out of the mountain of God in the presence of Moses. These are the Laws of God. They have been recognized by Christians and Jews for 3,300 years. They were 1,900 years old before The Prophet attempted to change them

What might it mean when the man who fulfilled all the characteristics of Lucifer comes to be known as the same man who fulfilled all the characteristics of *the little horn*? Might it raise a bit of concern to know that this man conquered the lands of Sheba and Dedan? He also pursued and conquered the merchants of the Tarshish – the caravanning tradesmen who traveled in these lands. This is the prophesied role of *the thief* who plundered and looted in the book of Ezekiel. Call it coincidence if you must, but the coincidences continue to pile upon him.

Stern-Faced Destruction
Daniel's descriptive warning of the Stern man (8:23-25)

In the book bearing his name, Daniel gives the reader another dimension of the Bible's ungracious villain. He describes this imminent menace as a strong, stern, and successful deviant whose artistry is demonstrated through deceit and devastating destruction. Daniel reminds us that this man, this stern-faced king, considers himself to be superior to all other men. He warns us about this undeserving king and how he will be the root cause of destruction for many peoples and nations. History has sided with Daniel's prophetic, Spirit-filled writing. The king's forewarned opposition to the Prince of princes (Jesus

Christ) is easily recognized and documented in readily available literature. The king's opposition to the Christ comes in nearly every form. One of these men is the Christ and the other is the antichrist. To anchor the point, the king opposed the Prince of princes by denying that He, Jesus, is the Son of God. Further, this self-appointed king has veiled his intriguing contempt by convincing many that his kingdom is built upon a foundation of 'peace.' Sadly, a lost and consciously ignorant world accepts the premise of this man's deceptions. The current and historical reality of the king's destructive endeavors is anything other than a patchwork of peace!

Six centuries after Jesus' crucifixion and five centuries after Jesus' prophets laid rest to their pens, this demonstrative fellow, he who Daniel describes as *the little horn*, was born and raised in the lands of Sheba and Dedan. He burst upon this desolate area at a time of woeful godlessness. A harlotous religion had previously taken root in the Roman Empire and its influence had been expanding for three centuries. Though the Romans called Jesus "Lord," they had adopted and incorporated their own cultural practices and mixed them with the Word to create something that Paul described as "demonic." They adored other gods and readily bowed to their man-made images. They carved angels out of wood and bowed before statues of *the Queen of Heaven*. They forbid their religious leaders from marrying and rejected Jesus' exception allowing for victimized divorcees to marry again. They ordered their followers to abstain from meat on certain days and they marked their faces in a manner advertising to the world that they were 'fasting.' Yet, they did not fast at all. They merely abstained from meat for a day and proclaimed to 'fast' from one behavior or another for 40 days. Like the Babylonians, they had taken up the golden cup and poured out abominations. Time after time, they made the claim that they were pouring the actual blood of Christ. Drunk by the potion of manmade tradition, they went mad. Such was a time when most had discarded the truth of the Father and His Son. With falsehoods abounding, the time was ripe for a new prophet and a different god. Enter the new king!

As a man, he was raised in the land that had become home to the resettled Jews. The Romans had scattered them from Jerusalem five centuries earlier. The Prophet took advantage of the drunken and adulterous behaviors of harlotous Rome. Confused by the self-imposed traditions of the Romans, people in the land were fascinated by the accusations of contradiction described by the little horn. He claimed that Christians honored the Father, Son, and 'Mother.' Of course, the truth is that Christians honor the Father, His Son, and His Spirit – while rejecting the adoration of any "Queen of Heaven." This Babylonian queen is the entity who claimed Jesus as her Groom while she committed adultery with the kings of the earth. With its political power and corporate greed, the body of the harlot abandoned the faith soon after the prophets had completed their writing. The harlot's diary reveals that The Prophet was to become one of her many partners. Without her man-made traditions and unrepentant disobedience, the accusations of the false prophet might have otherwise fallen on deaf ears. But in that day and in that land the brushstrokes of idolatry, false tradition, and lawlessness were among the many acts that painted a new picture of what was called *God*. With the harlot selling her wares in the land, the stage was set, and the time was right for a wayward merchant to execute many sins and institute his dishonest trade. Because men delighted in wickedness and refused to love the Truth, God sent them a powerful delusion. He sent them the master of intrigue. Here was a man with an evil scheme! Six hundred years after Jesus' paid the ransom for men, The Prophet appeared to discard Jesus' sacrifice and offering. This man would not honor any of the gods of his fathers before him. Though he boasts that his god is the god of Abraham, he speaks of a god unknown to the men and prophets before him. Instead, he honored a god of fortresses. In this time of man's wicked rebellion and his refusal to love the written and unchanging Truth, the world received and welcomed another. There are many who listened to his words and believed in what he said. These are a people who can no longer recognize their right hand from their left. They can no longer recognize the differences between The Prophet's god and God. For those who refused to love the truth and be saved, for those who have delighted in wickedness, a new prophet has appeared and reigned supreme. He brings with him dishonest trade. He has changed the laws. He promotes a woeful practice known as 'righteous murder.' He founded and instituted destruction by peace. Utilizing the deceit of counterfeit miracles and nearly every sort of deception, he attempted to change all that was written by the prophets before him. As is written, he…

- "… became very strong, but not by his own power." If the Holy Spirit of God guides and empowers His prophets, then who or what guides and empowers The Prophet? If we have come to know God by knowing Jesus, His speaking image, then we can know and recognize the foreign god by knowing his speaking image. The Son speaks for the Father by way of Word and Spirit. These two witnesses are in perfect agreement. Similarly, the Prophet speaks for the foreign god by way of word and spirit. But his word and spirit differ greatly from the Word and Spirit that preceded him. These two men, the Christ and the antichrist, speak in opposition to one another. The truth and grace of Jesus and his testimony reflects the image of God. The Prophet, now known as *the stern-faced king*, reflects the image of his god

- "… was a master of intrigue." And just what was this man's intrigue? He devised an evil scheme that opposed the Father and Son. He verbally expressed a covenant, an agreement, between his god and those who still refuse to love the truth. He spoke a covenant that was confirmed in the way of a book. His intrigue continues to this day. His followers continue to grow and gain power. His intrigue includes the destruction of many by his unique definition of 'peace.' His methods consist of strategic force and never-ending coercions that were built upon a foundation of war. After all, it was Satan's war in heaven that caused him to be hurled down to earth. In a like manner, it was war that caused Satan's speaking image, Lucifer, to fall from heaven to earth

- "… was stern-faced." Jesus is the gift of God who brought about forgiveness and grace. *Stern-face* is and was just that – stern! He taught his followers to pick up the stones of a new-found righteousness that Jesus taught men to drop. Though people are notorious for denying inconvenient facts, this one is impossible to deny. The Prophet gave his followers the directive to murder others for breaking his laws. This is confirmed in writing and cannot be reasonably disputed. It is by his direct order that his followers continue to sling those stones today. It is also by his account that the Towers were destroyed on September 11th. Yesterday's warning about *Stern-face* has become today's reality. His actions and directives have found their way into our everyday lives

- "… has become very strong." Although he's been dead for nearly 1400 years, his power and influence over our world is greater than ever and it continues to grow. His body of believers, the Prophetiers whose beliefs are founded on war, amounts to nearly two billion people. His nations and army have amassed weapons of mass destruction. With this, biblical prophecy has become an overwhelming reality. People have been fooled and misled. God warned that these things must happen. The Prophet was to hide in plain sight until all of God's prophecies were fulfilled. This wraps things up! We are told that "he will be revealed at the proper time." We see him now, so this can be none other than 'the proper time'

- "… has caused astounding devastation." The historical examples of his astounding devastation are highlighted by the events of 9/11. The whole world watched in horror as 19 of his disciples hijacked four commercial airliners and piloted them into the Twin Towers and the Pentagon. The fourth airliner had targets in Washington D.C. but was brought down, nose-first, into a field in Pennsylvania. May God Bless the heroic passengers who took a stand against the Prophetiers and their evil intentions. The motivation behind the attacks can be found within The Prophet's recorded directives. He warns that all hypocrites, those who refuse to abide by his changed laws, shall have "death overcome them, though they are in Towers, raised high." The Prophetiers attempted to topple these towers in 1993. Though their initial attempt to have death overcome those who are in Towers raised high fulfilled the thief's characteristics of killing and destroying, they failed in their endeavors to bring these buildings to the ground. Sadly, through their coordinated efforts on September 11, 2001, they succeeded. The Towers were only 35 years old. Stern-face's body of believers murdered nearly 3,000 people on that day. They did so to advance their envisioned form of 'peace'

- "… has succeeded" in instituting his plan. He is the founder and lone spokesman of the divergent evil that originated in his haunted mind. His is the name found at the top of the flowchart that dates back 14 centuries. Raining down from that name are the hordes of Prophetiers who can now be found in nearly every nation on earth, and they are seated amongst most governing bodies. They squad in the U.S. House of Representatives and continue to be as vocal as they are visual in their destructive mission. They make little effort to hide their hate of the American Dream while they spew unfiltered tirades of antisemitism

- "… has destroyed mighty men and holy people." The number of people that have been slaughtered to advance his cause are too numerous to calculate. Thanks to 14 centuries of his never-ending war, the number of dead and wounded might reach as high as hundreds of millions of people. So, how is it that so much death and destruction has been orchestrated by the demonic schemes of just one man and his people - without the world taking notice to his biblical identity? The only reasonable answer is that God chose for him to remain hidden until now

- "… has caused deceit to prosper and boasts that he is superior." Which of the biblical prophets is superior to another? The harlot will tell you that Peter is in the first position. Such are the babblings of a drunken prostitute! No prophet of God is superior to another. Even Jesus washed the feet of his brothers – both His literal and spiritual bothers. But not *Stern-face*! He claims that he is above them all. He claims that he is above Moses, Isaiah, Jeremiah, and Daniel. He claims that he is above Matthew, Mark, Luke, and John. He claims that he is above Jesus' post-ascension disciple Paul. Stern-face claims that he is above Jesus Christ

- "… destroys many when they feel secure." He taught his people to do as he did and make treaties with their enemies without the intent to abide by their agreements. He taught his people to befriend Christians and Jews only to "guard yourselves against them." The world refuses to accept that these tactics are still practiced in the 21st century. But these are among the deceptive tools used to subdue and defeat all who oppose him. Such are the acts of a man bent on conquering. A hopeful world cannot accept that honest peace can never be found with him or with the people he has deceived

- "… has destroyed many by peace." This contradictory statement is found within the KJV Bible. How can any man 'destroy by peace?' The answer is found within the man who created a movement that utilizes murder and destruction as the necessities of war and 'righteous deeds' in the pursuit of overcoming all previous beliefs and teaching. He defined peace as "fighting… until all religions are only for [his god]." We now understand how The Prophet's destruction by peace has become a horrific reality. His intrigue, this evil plan, is the world's real inconvenient truth. His version of peace now insures that "war will continue until the end." With so many followers and an escalating growth rate, how could it end any other way?

- "… has taken his stand against the Prince of princes." Daniel's prophetic life and inspired writing occurred five centuries before Jesus arrived. Jesus' prophetic life in the flesh and everlasting Word occurred six centuries prior to Stern-face's appearance. Referred to as the preincarnate *Prince of princes*, Jesus is the Prince opposed by Stern-face. The written evidence is unchangeable, historic, and woefully condemning for The Prophet

- "… will be destroyed, but not by human power." Stern-face died centuries ago. Unlike Jesus, this master of intrigue did not die by murder. His death is not accredited to any man or group of men. He died of a fever. Though he is long gone, his torment has likely already begun and will be ongoing. But his eternal destruction has not come about yet. Those who know God understand that our souls are not limited to the confines of our bodies. There comes a day when the body and soul are separated. In that day, some of us return to our Father who sent us. Others, those who delight in wickedness, are a part of man's rebellion. Those who take part in the rebellion never return to our Father above. They remain here, on earth, permanently removed from heaven. When God tells us that "war will continue until the end," He means it. War is what The Prophet continues to wage against the saints and the nations. His destruction and the destruction of all rebellious souls comes about in the second death

Is it all just a Fairy Tale or is there now enough proof? When proof of God is delivered by revealing the historical identity of the false prophet, how can a single Word of the Bible be rejected as the only hope of weak men? The written and historical evidence defining this one man as the biblical villain is astounding! But don't be deluded into thinking that his unveiling will change men's hearts and eliminate the threat. There are those, in fact most, whose ultimate arguments are misdirection and denial. For them, there is no mountain of evidence high enough to prove that God is God.

Chapter 3

After The Tax Collector

Daniel's warning of the man's appearance after the Roman Tax Collectors (11:20-33)

Once again, Daniel offers a multitude of would-be future figureheads and the kingdoms they would lead. What started with pen and parchment has since become history. The biblical community has largely understood the commentary of Daniel's 11th chapter to be the historical struggles between kingdoms leading up to the Romans and Caesar's infamous implementation of taxation to fund his empire. Jesus addresses this directly in His discussion about the image of Caesar on a Roman coin. Now keep in mind that Daniel lived during the Babylonian period – long before there was a Roman kingdom and its succession of god-like Caesars. The history leading to Rome's rule is wholly recognized and accepted to be biblically accurate. Inexplicably, most eschatologists overlook the massive nation that began to form in the dying days of the Roman Empire - the common thought being that some sort of a reborn Roman kingdom will emerge in the coming future. In the movie *Damien*, this reformed kingdom is represented as the European Union. But the kingdom that followed Rome was not something of Rome's own reformation. The kingdom that formed after Rome was founded by a single man. Though it has been weakened many times, it exists to this day, and it is larger and more powerful than ever before. The nation or kingdom was founded by The Prophet, he who fulfilled all the things of the contemptible thief who rose to power as a self-proclaimed prophet of God. He founded the seventh kingdom - that which followed the Roman Empire.

With a few like-minded outlaws, his rebellion expanded for over 20 years in his lifetime and culminated with an audience of 120,000 men and their families. That was almost 1,400 years ago. Their numbers now amount to approximately 1,800,000,000. The contemptible person who replaced Rome and its many Caesars is The Prophet. It is he who causes the left hand (god) to look like the right hand (God).

- The biblical Tax Collector collapsed under its own weight
- Historically, the contemptible person who succeeded Rome's Caesars was the stern-faced king described in Daniel 8
- Building his empire on a foundation of war, this new king created many enemies. With these enemies he agreed to and struck numerous treaties. However, his treaties were disingenuous. As is his teaching, these deceptive practices were a means to an end. They were intended to suspend the conflict or conflicts until his forces could manage an upper hand. The conflict would then resume. Lying, as it were, is just one of his many strategical tactics in an ongoing war against mankind
- With only a few like-minded thieves, The Prophet began his rise to power
- Unlike his fathers before him, this contemptuous person abandoned nearly 2,000 years of written and prophetic testimony about the God of Abraham and set about to change the record. To successfully pull off his intriguing endeavors, he declared that his god and the God of Abraham were one and the same.
- At the time of his death, there were 120,000 men and their families who could not tell their right hand from their left hand - they could not differentiate the God of Heaven from the god that this man introduced. If one was to ask about the difference between gods, they would likely hear the common, instinctive response that there is only one God. That would be correct. But they stop short of expanding on the warning about the liar and neglect Daniel's warning about the foreign god and John's teaching about the masquerading light – Satan
- The contemptible person's story begins with his plundering of Sheba, Dedan, and the merchants of the Tarshish. As his own testimony reveals, he stole from the people in these lands and distributed their plunder and wealth amongst his followers
- His heart was set against the holy covenant - God's Word. Remember, The Prophet set out to reject the testimonies of previous prophets, declaring their testimony to have been tainted over time
- His battles are numerous and mostly recorded within his own little book. Particularly interesting was a battle that did not go as planned and he was struck in the face by a rock - breaking his teeth. A rumor quickly spread of his death

- In what can only be described as a river of blood and a stack of bodies, The Prophet participated in the beheadings of hundreds of captive Jews. This recorded event came about because he believed they betrayed him, which led to setbacks and his being nearly defeated in battle. This tribe of Jews is among the people who participate in the holy covenant and are prophesied to receive God's inheritance. In this case, The Prophet certainly did not let his captives go home

- To understand the discussions about *covenants* it is important to note that God has formed a covenant with His people. In a like manner, the masquerading light has formed a covenant with his people. These are two very different covenants. The associated war between the two bodies is self-evident. God's covenant is holy. A reminder of His covenant is given to us in the way of a rainbow. Though this is a bit of a departure from the subject, it's important to understand the contempt that some people demonstrate when they worship a rainbow flag and the acts that it now represents. Whether it's the rainbow flag or images of the moon and stars, today's use of these symbolic idols demonstrates how rebellion comes in many forms

- Just 53 years after The Prophet's death, his armed forces rose-up to desecrate the Temple grounds in Jerusalem. It was on the Temple Mount that they dedicated an existing building to their prophet and god. The year was 685 A.D. This just happens to be 1,290 biblical years after the destruction of the first Jewish Temple. The abomination that stands on that ground is the cause of desolation today. Christian and Jewish prayers are forbidden and outlawed on the Temple Mount. Hence, it is the abomination that causes desolation. At the time of this writing, the abomination that causes desolation was dedicated 1,335 years ago

- Faithful Christians and practicing Jews know the prophetic, biblical God. As one body, they firmly resist The Prophet and the abomination that has been set up on the Temple Mount

History is a sound witness. Everything written above has historical reference or is currently ongoing. What could be more of an abomination than a foreign god, his false prophet and their symbolic idols of moon and star adorning the Temple Mount? It has been erected upon the ashes of what used to be the Jewish Temple in Jerusalem. Jesus once taught and prayed on that ground. His efforts and actions would be forbidden there today.

Ronald B. Stetton

The Prophet: Quick Notes

Chapter 4

Religious King Who Exalted Himself

Daniel's latter warning about the false prophet and his foreign god (11:36-45)

Without fail, Daniel follows through with his Spirited case against the man who introduced a foreign god and founded a kingdom based on war. The detailed warnings that Daniel gave us about this stern-faced king are over 2,500 years old and are now documented, historical accounts. More and more, with each fulfilled prophecy, the reader begins to understand the significance of the price that has been paid for redistributing conquered lands. After all, what value can be placed upon hundreds of millions of lives? Just as he redistributed stolen goods among his companions, The Prophet has effectively redistributed conquered lands among his followers.

In the following segment, Daniel gives us another set of characteristics and achievements that match up to the life and teaching of The Prophet. Can it really be nothing other than coincidence that *Stern-face* transitions into *the king who exalts himself*? Consider the following…

- The king did as he pleased. During his lifetime, The Prophet had at least thirteen documented wives and a concubine. Likely the most noted among his many wives was a nine-year-old girl. He stole for a living. He murdered those who interfered with his plans. He caused destruction everywhere he went – even stretching the bounds of time and extending his murderous directives to his many followers

- He exalted and magnified himself above all of God's prophets, raising his throne above all of them

- He said unheard of things about and against the God of gods. Chief among the things he said was that God is not a Father and that it would have been beneath God to have had a Son. How interesting it is to know that God had two witnesses – His Son and His Spirit. These three (Father, Son & Spirit) agree as one. They are different but inseparable. This might be a bit difficult to grasp but it becomes a little more clear when one reads Isaiah's description of the Preincarnate Jesus. "For to us a child is born, to us a Son is given, and the government will be on His shoulders. And He will be called Wonderful Counselor, Mighty God, Everlasting Father, Prince of Peace." Isaiah called Jesus the *Everlasting Father*. Now it might prove to be a little easier to understand Jesus' statement that knowing Him is knowing His Father. They are one. But The Prophet has another tale to tell. He talks of the light (his god) who refuses to claim a son. Those who know God understand that He will not be defamed. He will not yield His glory to the rebellious acts of the liar. This is what caused war in heaven. This is the root cause of the longest lasting war on earth. The Prophet gives God's glory to the masquerading light, Satan, he who was cast from heaven with his dark angels for their woeful rebellion

- He has succeeded in all that he has done - until now. Members of his body have been selected and placed into some of the highest offices of the most powerful nations on earth. But the deceit of his endeavors is nearly over. All that remains is his unveiling. To evaporate the fog of delusion surrounding him and remove his ability to hide in plain sight, all of prophecy must be fulfilled. The proper time to reveal this man as the most evil ever to exist is when his words and actions can be matched to biblical warnings. That time seems to have arrived

- He showed no regard for the gods of his fathers – none

- He showed no regard for the Messiah – He who is desired by women. This is not to be mistaken for sexual desire. Jesus changed the world when He stood between the prostitute and her self-righteous judges. In that moment, Jesus taught men to recognize our own shortcomings and drop our stones of righteous and lethal judgment. No man is worthy of instituting a lethal sentence upon another. After all, how can a sinner judge and condemn another sinner? This is the graceful teaching of the true *bright Morning Star*. Jesus' lesson is contrary to the teaching of the self-exalted king. And what of that odd statement about 'the desire of women'? The reader is urged to consider the extent to which any woman might desire the actions and traditions of the man who is ultimately responsible for female mutilation, assault, oppression, and unspeakable abuses. With Afghanistan as the latest example, this needs little more explanation

- There were many gods worshiped in the lands of Sheba & Dedan during the rise of this self-exalted king. Least among them was Jesus. But, surviving the false traditions growing among the Romans, the Way of Christ stood firm in the unchanged writing of the prophets. Understanding that Jesus is the speaking image of His Father and that the self-exalted king denies them as one God, it is reasonable to deduce that this king exalts himself above God and His Word. Jesus walked the earth and was crucified nearly 600 years before the self-exalted king appeared and died. Therefore, Jesus was among the gods of the The Prophet's fathers. The Prophet's rejection of Jewish, Christian, and Roman deities is clearly documented. His inability to separate the Word of God from false Roman traditions is easily recognized among faithful Christians when pointed out

- Recognizing God's Word and understanding His Laws was easily attained by the prophets of God. All of them could read and write. But such was not the case for The Prophet. This self-exalted king could not read Moses' testimony about Abram's son, Ishmael, and Abraham's son Isaac. Ishmael's lineage has most certainly lived up to the warning "…his hand will be against everyone and everyone's hand against him, and [his lineage] will live in hostility toward all of his brothers." There should be little confusion as to how the self-exalted king advanced this prophecy to its ultimate fulfillment. With the Ishmaelites destined to become men of violence and war, there is no biblical evidence or indication that any prophet of God ever originated from that vine

- Instead of honoring the God of his fathers, this king honored a god of fortresses - a god unknown to his fathers. He gave testimony to this fact. He addressed his body of believers as *fortresses*. When a man builds a religion on the foundation of war and calls his followers fortresses, the strange statement "…he will honor a god of fortresses" begins to make sense. Further, when he was confronted about his teaching and telling many to believe in the revelations of his god over the god of their fathers, he responded: "What! Even though their fathers had no sense at all, nor did they follow the right way"

Consider the price already paid in the way of injuries and deaths. Think about how many people have died and how many are still to die in the name of the god of fortresses. How could the price be any higher? How high might it go?

Ronald B. Stetton

Chapter 5

Seeing The Abomination That Causes Desolation

Unveiling the warnings of Daniel 9 & Matthew 24

The simplicity of this chapter is awe-inspiring. Most of those who know the Father and His Son firmly believe that they will recognize the abomination when they see it. However, this abomination has been standing in plain sight for centuries. As it is written, the abomination stands where it does not belong. It stands there now. Thankfully, men can come to understand what the abomination is and how it was set up. In the simplest of terms, abomination is seen as something wicked or vile – like worshiping a god other than God. Abomination is accepting the loathsome testimony of one contradictory prophet over the congruent testimony of the Father's two witnesses. The Spirit of God is what guided the pen of every true prophet of God before the appearance and intrigue of The Prophet. All of God's prophets agree upon the eternal Word and Law of the Father. Nothing about their written testimony ever changes. That is, not until the appearance of the harlot and The Prophet she desires. In her drunken stupor, she is blind to the abomination he inspired!

Abomination is an accepted departure from all that is agreed to and written in the image of God. Abomination is departure from God's Law. Abomination is setting up a house of worship for the foreign god and his lone prophet. Abomination is found atop the ruins of the Jewish temple - that which currently sits on the Temple Mount. The abomination was set up by The Prophet's hordes under the power of the speaking image of the foreign god. Seeing the abomination for what it is, where it is, the reader can now understand how the king who exalted himself has succeeded in building his nefarious rebellion in plain sight. His mischievous plan includes keeping God's elect (Christians and Jews) from praying upon the Temple Mount in Jerusalem. That slight piece of ground is currently desolate of prayer between men and God. Hence, it is literally 'the abomination that causes desolation.' And, instead of prayers emanating from the Temple Mount (an obvious wing of the temple), men now hear the roar of the seven thunders.

Ronald B. Stetton

Chapter 6

Sound of Seven Thunders

John's warning about the seven "Oft-repeated" verses (Revelation 10)

Complementing Daniel's writing, John wrote the book of *Revelation*. When the book of Revelation is condensed into evidentiary bits, much of John's vivid imagery begins to paint a picture of a very familiar character and his god. For instance, everyone knows that thunder accompanies lightning. Lightning is the visual image we are given when Jesus describes how He saw Satan fall from heaven. As an extension of this image, John describes the masterful lies or sounds of Satan as 'thunders.' To the eyes, the sight of Satan is like lightning. To the ears, the sound of Satan is like thunder.

Chief among these thunders are the seven guiding principles that form the foundation of the covenant between the Lightning (Satan) and the hordes of The Prophet's followers - his deceived body. These seven are the opening sounds in the first chapter of Satan's little book. Daniel refers to these seven thunders as 'one seven' in Daniel chapter 9. Remember that Daniel wrote as a prophet of God 600 to 700 years before John was called to prophesy.

Called the *oft-repeated verses,* these seven statements or seven thunders make up the sound of Lightning – the fallen angel. They are the seven summary statements chanted repeatedly by the fallen angel's body of believers. With this body now numbering almost two billion people, these seven thunders create a bit of a roar in the way of daily prayers. The announcement or *call to prayer* is often resonated among their many communities by way of loudspeaker. This sound is unmistakable.

The verse in the middle of the *'seven'* is the woeful statement that puts an end to the gift of God's selfless act of sacrifice and offering. Further reference to this is found in Daniel 9:27. The meaning of this warning is that the fallen angel, Satan, takes away God's gift to mankind by convincing many to reject Jesus and, instead, look to the liar for help. Of course, those who act in such a manner believe they are trusting in God. This is the deception. This is the rebellious rejection of God's gift and paid ransom. In this single statement, the powerful angel succeeds in ending the sacrifice and offering of God (the life of His Son) for many. The 'many' that Daniel speaks of amounts to billions of people. Hidden among the roars of the seven thunders is the Lightning's successful removal of the ransom paid by Jesus' selfless act. Jesus' faithful followers have no reason to be alarmed. Satan cannot remove the gift of God from His elect. The liar can only end the benefits of Jesus' act for those who refuse to love the truth. They bend their knees and roar in honor of the masquerading light – he who was the original source of the seven thunders. The dark warning that Daniel wrote 25 centuries ago has now been dragged into the light for all to see.

Chapter 7

Revelation Before the Day Of The Lord

Paul's warning about the man of lawlessness (2 Thessalonians 2)

Admittedly, there is much confusion among Christians about Paul's statements in the second chapter of his second letter to the Thessalonians. But trusting in the Word, and reading it with the simplicity in which it is written, removes any doubt.

"Concerning the coming of our Lord Jesus Christ and our being gathered to Him… that day will not come until the rebellion occurs and the man of lawlessness is revealed."

In other words, Jesus' return and our being gathered to Him will not happen until the man of lawlessness is revealed. We are talking about The Prophet who claimed that God's Laws were outdated. Now, consider the great weight of Paul's statement. The only thing holding back Christ's return is man's recognition of the man of lawlessness! Be ready for his return!

Unlike common expectations, mankind is not waiting for the son of perdition to suddenly appear. We are not waiting for a new Jewish temple to be built on the Temple Mount. We are not waiting for a seven-year treaty to be struck between the Antichrist and Israel. We are not waiting for seven more years of tribulation. We are waiting for one thing and one thing only. We are waiting for the unveiling of the man of lawlessness. Men have waited to see which prophet would take it upon himself and try to change God's unchanging Laws. We waited for a prophet to oppose and exalt himself over everything that is called *God*. We waited for the opposer, Lucifer, to appear and give himself Jesus' honorable title as the *bright Morning Star*. We waited for the antichrist prophet who "snipes the necks" of those who refuse to obey his changed laws. We waited for the unveiling of The Prophet whose demands and directives would lead to the oppression and abuse of women, so egregious that it now accommodates sexual mutilation. We waited to learn the identity of The Prophet who was first to speak the covenant summarized by the seven thunders of Lightning. We waited to learn who would prove to be the speaking image of *the first beast*.

If God is God and if He gave us the end from the beginning, then proof of God must come in irrefutable form. That proof now comes by way of The Prophet and his god. We now know that 'the mystery of God will be accomplished, just as He announced to His servants the prophets.' With these mysteries unveiled, how can we not share these findings with our families? How can we not share these findings with our friends? How can we refuse to be good ministers of Christ Jesus and neglect sharing this evidence with our brothers in the faith?

There is one man who has succeeded in all things that define the man of lawlessness…

- …He declared himself to be a prophet of God. The menacing voice in his head never identified itself as *Gabriel*. That misnomer originated with The Prophet's first wife's uncle. He was the "prophet" who mistook Gabriel for the angel that guided Moses. But the only angel named in the story of Moses is *Michael*.

- …He set himself up on a wing of the temple – as part of the abomination that causes desolation on the Temple Mount

- …He set himself up in God's temple – as the *lamp of light*

- …He proclaimed to be God – as the *lamp of light* and *bright morning star*

- …He changed the Laws of God – as *the little horn* & *son of perdition*

- …He created the rebellion that teaches people to worship the masquerading light (Lightning) as God with counterfeit miracles, signs, and wonders

- …He introduced every sort of evil as forms of worship – cowardice, unbelieving in Father & Son, vile behavior, murder, sexual immorality, false miracles, idolatry, and the artistry of lies

Every warning about the coming of the lawless one has been satisfied by The Prophet. Every warning about the coming of the body of the lawless one has been satisfied by the many billions who will perish because they refuse to love the truth.

Remember the 4th thunder as it is roared by The Prophet's hordes. As a collective body, they roar their rejection of God's gift and, instead, seek help from the fallen angel. "For this reason, God sent them a powerful delusion so that they will believe the lie and so that all will be condemned who have not believed the truth but have delighted in wickedness." Can there be a greater example of 'delighting in wickedness' than those who celebrated the horrific acts of September 11, 2001? They see such wickedness as the dutiful acts of a necessary war. And, because of them, there will be war until the end. And the end of the war comes with the unveiling of The Prophet. He loses…

Chapter 8

Antichrist Prophet

John's definitive warning about the Antichrist (1 John 2)

Wave after wave of ominous and contemptuous evidence continues to build in the case against this biblical villain. What began as a smoldering mole hill has now become a blazing mountain. Utilizing the most basic of biblical definitions, the reader can agree that an antichrist is anyone who denies the Father and His Son. Unlike God's chosen people, those who know God as a Father, the antichrist has created a massive movement, a rebellion, that denies the Father and the Son. Instead, they delight in a god who sees the role of father as undignified and beneath him.

God's body of believers understands that the foreign god is one of many names - not the least of which is the father of lies. No matter the reader's opinion on religious faith and what they might consider to be God, the definition of *antichrist* is a Christian term that cannot be altered. Not even the P.C. crowd can twist this one. The term *antichrist* identifies those who refute God's role as a Father. The word *antichrist* is rooted in biblical terms with precise intent. John introduced and defined the term *antichrist* in the second chapter of his first book. Whether one believes in the Christ or antichrists is irrelevant when it comes to the intentional definition of the term. Therefore, by definition, anyone who says or agrees that "The Beneficent has no Son" is an antichrist. What conclusion can we then make of The Prophet who made this very statement? What reasonable conclusion can we come to about The Prophet's body of believers who believe what he taught? It's elementary! According to the definition, The Prophet is and was an antichrist. According to the definition, the Prophetiers (his hordes) are antichrists.

This is certainly going to make the P.C. crowd gnash their teeth!

Ronald B. Stetton

Chapter 9

The Speaking Image

John's description of the false prophet (Revelation 13)

Jesus tells us, "I am the way and the truth and the life. No one comes to the Father except through me. If you really knew me, you would know my Father as well. From now on, you do know Him and have seen Him." That makes Jesus the speaking image of His Father. What, then, can be said of the antichrist prophet who delivered the foreign god's covenant and spoke his seven thunders? Is it reasonable to assume that the antichrist is the speaking image of *his* father? This comparison might seem to be overly simplistic but there is no denying that Jesus speaks as His Father speaks. His Word and Laws remain written and without change. No change. God's Laws are still God's Laws. Jesus did not come to change one letter of God's Laws. But we now know that The Prophet, the villainous orator, and the speaking image of the first beast, spoke like the dragon. He attempted to change God's Laws. He instructed and continues to instruct his followers to snipe the necks of those who refuse to follow his changed laws. He speaks the native language of his father - *the first beast*. He lies. He was a murderer from the beginning. It's easy to understand how the lines become gray as to who 'he' is - the dragon or his speaking image? Aside from the flesh, is there any difference? If you really knew him, you would know his father as well.

For the moment, consider *the first beast* as another name for Satan. Daniel describes this beast in the 7th chapter of the book titled in his name. This helps the reader in separating the body of Satan, *the beast out of the sea*, from Satan himself. It was Satan, the dragon, who gave authority to his body of believers. That body consisted of the eight kingdoms from the time of Egypt to the present. These kingdoms (Egypt, Assyria, Babylon, Medo-Persia, Greece, Rome, and the kingdom of The Prophet) are vividly described as 'heads.' The head that was wounded was *Babylon*. How do we know this? We know this because Babylon is described as flourishing across the entire earth in the days prior to the apocalypse. Though Babylon appeared to be fatally wounded and a thing of the past, it is alive and well in the two religions that have formed and taken root since the Ways of Christianity. Babylon is rooted in these two false, post-Christian deceptions. They are their own king and queen. Revelation 13 and *the beast out of the earth* become much easier to understand with these things in mind.

The first beast (Satan) predates *the beast out of the earth* (Lucifer). The beast out of the earth is the speaking image of Satan – with Satan being the dragon. As it is written, the speaking image of the dragon utilizes the dragon's power. Therefore, *the beast out of the earth,* he who speaks like the dragon, is Satan's speaking image. He is the image of the beast who gave breath to the covenant described in Daniel 9:27. That image is now summarized in a little book. That little book was written in the image of the dragon and biblical reference to it can be found in the warning of Revelation 10. There we see the fallen angel holding the little book in his hand. Most will cringe at this, but it's worthy of thought. How could God give us the end from the beginning and leave out the little book that leads so many people astray? God did not forget to tell us about The Prophet, his foreign god, their hordes, or their own little book. The challenge was keeping it all hidden in plain sight for so long.

As the reader now knows, many people worship the fallen angel as God. So, be prepared. They and many like them will proclaim it to be offensive and hateful to introduce these biblical warnings as historical facts. God and His Word is not very popular in this kingdom. People gnash their teeth and point their fingers of accusation at God's elect. God's elect are called 'hateful' for their love of the truth. Their children are called hateful. They use these accusations as the effective tactics of war. Take note of their reactions when they learn that billions of people have been lost to the delusional lessons of The Prophet. In a politically correct world, revealing the false prophet will not be as grand an achievement as one might think. Remember the lesson about the narrow and wide gates. God's people are greatly outnumbered. So, put on your armor and get ready for the arrows that will be flung. They are used with the intent to shut the conversation down. This, too, is of biblical prophecy.

The Prophet: Quick Notes

Chapter 10

Shorts

Victimizing Sheba & Dedan

Ezekiel's warning about the false prophet (38:10-13)

The book of Ezekiel compliments Daniel's warning about *the little horn*. Specifically, Ezekiel tells us how a marauding bandit will set himself upon the people of Sheba and Dedan (modern day Arabia) while stealing from a maritime people of the Mediterranean (the merchants of the Tarshish) and its surrounding lands. According to Ezekiel's testimony, the boastful thief performed these exact deeds in these exact places! However, The Prophet twists the telling of these accounts and justifies his life as a thief to be the actions of a holy man. He declares his acts of thievery to be righteous deeds, making him out to be some sort of godly hero – a Robin Hood among the prophets. The reality is that Robin Hood is a mythical character who did not boast about being a murderer and rapist. He did not boast about murdering his neighbors while enslaving their wives and children. Robin Hood never hailed himself a hero while setting himself upon Christians and Jews and raiding their unwalled villages. Robin Hood did not boast about sniping the necks of the inhabitants who resettled in the land. To the contrary, The Prophet stood in rivers of blood stemming from the necks he 'smited' in the interests of his own cause. The realities are that Robin Hood is a myth and The Prophet is entirely too real.

Body Of Believers

So many Led Astray

The Prophet could not have succeeded in his endeavors without a lot of help. It would take a large body of loyal believers (hordes) to become the largest nation on the planet. God calls these hordes *Hamon*. Hamon Gog are the hordes (Magog) of Gog (The Prophet), and Hamonah is the crowded town – Bakkah. This cringeworthy bit of information has become possible with the evaporation of babel. Accurate translations have revealed many truths!

The murder and mayhem that began in Sheba and Dedan has spread across the globe. Billions of people have fallen victim to this man and the institution of his lethal 'peace.' Nation after nation has succumbed to The Prophet's delusional prophecies and his blasphemies against the Father and His Son. The powers of politics have acted as resilient allies in his war against God and His people. Although common names are purposely avoided, the evidence offered on the Prophetiers is as absolute as it is self-evident. So overwhelming is the evidence against them that even the most politically correct among us cannot reasonably deny its accuracy. In no way does this suggest that the world will learn to love the truth. They won't. Instead, they will continue to revel in their love of hating the truth and delight in the wickedness of The Prophet and his biblically predicted deceptions. The whole world has been led astray.

Thief

Jesus' nemesis was a literal thief (Ezekiel 38:13 & 1 John 10)

It is as simple as it is written. The biblical menace was a literal thief. Jesus tells us that He, the Messiah, came to give us life and give it in full. But He warns that the thief comes only to steal and to kill and to destroy. Historical accounts and boastful recordings of this man's life and attitude add to the mountain of evidence against him. A thief is a thief is a thief. And this man tells us that he lived and died as a thief.

He literally began his life of armed robbery in the lands of Sheba and Dedan – stealing primarily from the merchants of the Tarshish. In his day, the caravans that traveled throughout Sheba and Dedan originated from the merchant vessels that traveled from country to country, across the Mediterranean and Red Seas. Once they arrived at their ports of destination, they caravanned their wares to individual cities from Egypt to Dedan; from Dedan to Sheba; and from Sheba to Damascus. These were the land-routes terrorized by history's most notorious thief. Today, many recognize him as the perfect model for men.

Fallen

Differentiating Lucifer from Satan (Isaiah 14)

One of the many factors that continues to confuse people about the difference between Lucifer and Satan is that both spirits have fallen. Most men recognize fallen to be the exclusive feature of Satan. But John tells us that 'many' of Satan's demons were thrown from heaven to earth. One of those demons was the spirit of Satan's speaking image – The Prophet. It is reasonable to accept that we can now trust Isaiah's written word. With Lucifer's position filled, the balance of Isaiah's testimony can be seen as faithful and true. Though we are products of the earth as flesh and blood, our souls are the product of God above. As per the testimony, a few souls return to the Father – from whom they originate. However, the greater portion, those who travel through the wide gate, remain here for eternity.

Jesus, the man, has risen. Lucifer, the man, has fallen. Each of these men speak in a manner that represents their fathers. Jesus speaks in the image of our Father above and Lucifer speaks in the image of his father – the father of lies. Jesus testifies that murder is against the Law of His Father and is sinful. Lucifer testifies that murder is a duty of necessity and a means of earning ones' way into paradise. Jesus promises that with Him comes life and a life to the full. Lucifer proclaims that holiness derives from being submissive and open to murder, theft, and destruction.

Sometimes, standing too close to an image can cause it to become blurred and unclear. But, by stepping back and visualizing the whole picture, the image comes into focus, and we see what was meant to be seen from the beginning. With the image of Lucifer clearing, the reality of who and what constitutes his god is certain to shake the earth.

Jerusalem Unmatched

The Promise of Revelation 21

Jerusalem is the city God loves. The reader likely recognizes Jerusalem to be a tiny sliver of land in Israel that remains a symbol of conflict and controversy. But Israel (God's people) and Jerusalem (the city) belong to God. God promised that Jerusalem would be a cup of trembling for all the surrounding peoples. It was trembling when the Jews settled there. It was trembling when the seven kingdoms conquered it. It was trembling when the temples were destroyed and when the Crusades took place. Jerusalem was a cup of trembling in the day of its rebirth and again in 1967. It is a cup of trembling in this moment. That is the place where the abomination that causes desolation has been set up.

It's been over 3,300 years since the Hebrews resettled in Jerusalem and it remains the cup of trembling that God promised it would be. But the earthly representation of Jerusalem, that cup of trembling, is not the New Jerusalem spoken of by John in the book of Revelation. Written 2,000 years ago, John described the New Jerusalem in nearly unimaginable proportions. Instead of the two-dimensional segment of land (48 square miles) recognized today, John describes the New Jerusalem as a three-dimensional kingdom, occupying a space of nearly three trillion 'cubic' miles. It is as high and wide as it is long. Such a place does not and never will exist on this earth. As Jesus says, "My kingdom is not of this world," and He meant it!

There is biblical reference made to an eternal hell that will be suffered by the devil, the devil's body (his people), and The Prophet. That woeful hell is described as a place of permanent torment - day and night. Few take the time to think it through, but the one place that experiences day and night is found only upon a revolving planet – like earth. This earth is the eternal destination for the condemned. This is where Satan and his demons were hurled down to perish. They are among the fallen. They never leave this place. Never...

Succeeding In Terror

Isaiah's warning about he who causes terror (Chapter 47)

In a post-Jesus world, any utilization of terrorists acts or lethal tactics for the advancement of any cause should be a dead giveaway that the causer is evil. By His Word, those who terrorize others simply cannot belong to God. Having a better life and having it in full leaves out the ridiculous notion that murder can somehow be 'weaved into the fabric our nation' as an improvement. Terror is a weapon utilized by Satan. Any man who would attempt to introduce such antichrist strategies into the teaching of God certainly does not know God. Without repentance, such a man certainly cannot be a part of God or be a part of God's kingdom.

In His mockery of Satan, God states, "Perhaps you will succeed, perhaps you will cause terror." God was correct. Satan has succeeded in causing terror. Via the efforts of his speaking image, Satan has instituted the use of terror into a rapidly growing nation. It should come as no surprise that the dragon's seventh statement, his seventh roar of thunder, speaks in opposition to God's Judeo-Christian prophets and those who find their teaching faithful and true. Repulsed by the perceived weaknesses of grace and forgiveness, The Prophet and his people demonstrated a stern type of self-righteousness so egregious that they were driven to demolish the Twin Towers and the people that were in them. The murder and destruction that came with that act is in accordance with the devil and the man who spoke the devil's counterfeit miracles – those miracles being found within the binding of the little book. The man who spoke like the dragon is the thief who came only to steal and to kill and to destroy. His use of terror is aligned with the methods of his father, he who was a murderer from the beginning. Sadly, these terror tactics are effective. They continue to this day. Some are so gruesome that the perpetrators are ruled to be mentally incompetent and unable to stand trial. This is the model of their perfection! Centuries of coercion and lethal manipulation have advanced The Prophet and his evil scheme. He has attempted and largely succeeded in stealing the glory of God and giving that glory to the liar. For obvious reasons, the world fears these murderous thugs and their callous endeavors. But their time is short. They are being dragged into the light for all to see.

Our World Led Astray

John's warning about the war that started in heaven (Revelation 12)

The world and its people have asked a great question: Why would God create such a villainous man and support him with a group of hideous murderers? The answer is simple: God created the man, but he warned of this and other rebellions. He did not create the lies that drive them. That's the liar's role. God warned us of their rebellion against Him. He warned us of the war in heaven that has spilled over to war here on earth. He tells us that "war will continue until the end." Wickedness and wanton rebellion brought about the grand delusion of The Prophet and his intriguing schemes.

Freedom of religion is a wonderful thing! But what happens when those freedoms are given to a murderous thug? Is freedom of religion to be granted to those who teach that anyone who opposes The Prophet and his god should be 'murdered?' Thanks to such freedoms, no matter how vile the teaching might be, The Prophet has found refuge in the world. This is the story of man. It's the story of man's rebellion and its generation of godless people. We now live in an environment of political correctness so deluded with entitlements that the speaking image and his people have succeeded in becoming the largest nation on the planet. Their intent is geared toward the nefarious teaching of their prophet and god.

The arguments are coming. Many will argue that the largest religion belongs to those who teach that Jesus is Christ – the Messiah. But these same people fail to acknowledge that half of those who call Jesus "Lord, Lord" are a part of the body of the harlot. Though they boast of being the bride of Christ, they refuse to obey His commands. His commands adhere to His Father's Laws. The Laws never change. But the harlot has her own needs and desires. Her loyalists have chosen to follow the teaching of demons and forsake the ways of Christ. They are lovers of the queen. Never to be mistaken for our mother, the free Jerusalem above, the queen of Revelation directs her body of believers to do the detestable and worship the woeful. She serves her biblical role by supporting things taught by demons – even the demonic prophet – declaring that his deluded body of believers is included in the plan of salvation. The demonic teaching of CCC 841 cannot be erased by the queen or her loyalists. Through her teaching and by way of her own little book, she advances The Prophet's notion that the masquerading light is God. The harlot's man-made traditions and love of money have caused her people to abandon the faith and follow things taught by demons. For these departures from the Way of Christ, she has earned her own biblical warnings. But, unless otherwise noted, her practices are a diversion from The Prophet and his endeavors. As such, her prophetic antics will be left for another day and another book.

It is a true wonder how two of the world's largest religions invoke the name of *Jesus Christ* but refuse to love His truth. These two post-Christian rebellions have grown to unimaginable dimensions. So large is the body of this woman and the body of the beast she rides that their current numbers account for three in every six adults who still take a breath on this planet. They are among the multitude who reject the Word of God and travel through the wide gate to their own destruction.

Plague of Frogs

John's warning about the false prophet, his god & army (Revelation 16:12-14)

Most people know or have heard about the plague of frogs suffered by the Egyptians prior to the Exodus of the Hebrews from Egypt. That plague was instituted by God to pressure Pharaoh into releasing his captives. But there is more to the story about a plague of frogs – something most people miss. The plague comes about again, but it does not originate in Egypt and the frogs are not literal. By way of magic arts, Pharaoh's magicians were able to bring frogs onto the land. Why would they bring this curse upon themselves? What good would these counterfeit miracles do for them? It seems that they merely multiplied their own troubles. With the current pandemic emanating from Wuhan and its laboratories, it seems that the world is unable or unwilling to learn from the lessons of plague. What then, shall we gather from the demonic spirits performing miraculous signs in the day of apocalypse?

- What comes out of the mouth of the dragon?
  Answer: It is an evil spirit that looks like plague

- What comes out of the mouth of his speaking image - The Prophet?
  Answer: It is an evil spirit that looks like plague

- What comes out of the mouth of their body of believers?
  Answer: It is an evil spirit that looks like plague

- Where does this take place?
  Answer: It takes place around the Euphrates River

- What is on either side of the Euphrates river?
  Answer: Syria and Iraq host the Euphrates

- Who are the kings to the East of the Euphrates River?
  Answer: These are Persian kings

- What are they doing?
  Answer: They are gathering the kings of the whole world for the battle on the great day of God Almighty.

- And, just to be clear, what gathers them there?
  Answer: They are gathered there because of the plague, the seven thunders, that comes out of the mouth of the masquerading light, out of the mouth of The Prophet, and out of the mouths of their hordes or body.

It takes little effort to remind the reader about the ongoing battles that have taken place in Syria, Iraq, and Iran in the last three decades. It no longer takes much effort to describe and recognize the evil spirits that have come out of the mouth of *Satan*, his speaking image *Lucifer,* and their body of believers – those who have vowed to wage war until the end. This biblical warning cannot be avoided and is now encased in the teaching of The Prophet.

In October of 2011, Baraq Hussein announced the removal of American troops from the region of the great river Euphrates. The vacuum he created by the sudden departure of the U.S. Military was immediately filled by the most vicious combat group ever assembled in the name of any foreign god. Their murderous rampages have not been limited to the geographical confines of the regions around the Great Euphrates. The events we see and the events we are soon to see are the direct result of the evil spirits that have come out of the mouth of the devil; out of the mouth of The Prophet; and out of the mouth of their menacing armies. In its efforts to placate to Hamon Gog, mankind has sealed its fate.

Beheaded Because of Testimony to the Word and The Son

John's warning about beheaded Christians (Revelation 20:4)

Promising to cause terror, the speaking image of the liar directs his body to 'snipe the necks' of those who disbelieve in his revelations and laws. This directive, to snipe the necks of their enemies, is consistent with the directive to kill the hypocrites, 'though they are in Towers, raised high.' These murderous lessons are recorded and have been pressed upon the minds of many people for centuries. The times might have changed, but the directives remain the same. Recognizing these actions as religious duties, many people willingly carry them out with their own hands, and those who do not act in such a way are duty bound to support those who do. It should be noted that those who "give testimony to Jesus and recognize the Word of God" are named enemies of The Prophet and his Prophetiers. Befriending Christians and Jews is strictly forbidden unless they do so for strategic purposes. Once again, men are entitled to their opinions on this matter, but the historical examples, documented lessons, and ongoing acts amount to irrefutable evidence that Jesus' biblical nemesis has already made his mark upon men.

Peace and Safety

Paul's warning about those who falsely espouse "peace" (1 Thessalonians 5)

In a glance, it's hard to make sense out of Paul's warning that destruction comes upon those who say, "Peace and safety." Why would God promote the destruction of those who profess to peace? The answer is now vivid. The Prophet's vision of 'peace' is used as the ultimate deception. This is the work of the stern-faced king and his tactical manipulation of righteous terror. Of course, there is no such thing as righteous terror. It exists only in the minds of the deluded. The reality of The Prophet's promised 'peace' is found trampled in worthless treaties, buried under billions of victims, bulldozed over destroyed homelands, and negated by endless wars.

The greeting exchanged between Hamon Gog (the Prophetiers) is, "Peace and security!" What began as a battlefield code-phrase in the days of the warring prophet has become the traditional greeting between members of The Prophet's fallen kingdom. It is a ruse – a manner and method of 'peace' in which his body has been able to advance their schemes and destroy those who disagree. The inconvenient truth about this world has nothing to do with global warming or the more inclusive term of 'climate change.' Man's inconvenient truth is that The Prophet is an historical character who set the example to snipe the necks of those who reject his rules and laws. His example of lethal judgment remains and is one of the reasons why we read so many Headlines about the Prophetiers and the horrible things they have done. These are The Prophet's lessons about peace and security. And this is what is soon to be destroyed.

Ronald B. Stetton

The Prophet: Quick Notes

Chapter 11

The Odds

A numeric demonstration about the one man who has fulfilled this villainous role

Though no man can accurately portray the odds of The Prophet being the biblical villain, we can utilize the minds of brilliant men to better visualize the realm of possibility surrounding the fulfillment of prophetic occurrences. For example: Peter W. Stoner wrote that the mathematical probability that any man might fulfill just eight biblical prophecies about the coming Messiah is 1 in 100,000,000,000,000,000 (1 X 10^{17}). Jesus fulfilled those eight prophecies and all others relating to the His coming. Since most of us lack the ability to process such a number, Mr. Stoner offered an image that better portrays those odds. He asks the reader to visualize silver dollars spread out over the entire state of Texas. To reach his number of 10^{17}, he says that the dollars would need to be about two feet deep. He then asks the reader to imagine marking an "X" on just one of those dollars and mixing the entire batch. Now, he says, blindfold a man and send him walking in any direction he wants for as long as he'd like to walk and reach into the heap of dollars in hopes of selecting that one coin. The odds say it can't happen. Obviously, that would be impossible. Jesus' very existence as the Messiah is therefore verified by the science of probability.

In another example, the odds of winning the Mega-Millions Lottery is quite attainable in comparison at just 1 in 10^7! Now, we're not mathematicians nor can we reasonably utilize the science of probability to predict the odds of The Prophet fulfilling all 65+ listed prophecies about the biblical villain. But we can do simple math and consider the odds of blindly selecting eight numbered Ping-Pong balls in ascending order. There are over 40,000 (4 X 10^4) different combinations that these Ping-Pong Balls can be retrieved. That's substantially easier to achieve than Peter Stoner's chance of 10^{17} for Jesus fulfilling just eight prophecies. Using the simpler math, what are the odds of retrieving 65 Ping Pong Balls in ascending or descending order? Most of your calculators won't go there and the boredom will make you crazy! But the odds of retrieving just the first 10 of the 65 in either ascending or descending order is 6.5 X 10^{17}! And there would still be 55 more to retrieve! What, then are the odds of any man fulfilling all 65 prophecies about being the biblical bad guy? The only reasonable answer is that it is impossible for any man to do so - unless he is, in fact, *that man*. Therefore, it would seem, that it is finished. There cannot be another. God's Word does not make allowances for a second such perpetrator. Why would it? The Prophet is not only a historical figure, but the math tells us that his existence and his fulfillment of prophecy is verifiable proof of God.

Chapter 12

The Whole World Waits

We have arrived

The whole world waits...

We wait to see if there is a God. We wait to see if His biblical Word gave us the accurate end from the beginning. We've been offered the story of man by way of the Word, the Son of God, He who was with God in the beginning. We have received a prophetic compilation of over 60 books and letters, written by more than 40 authors who lived and died some 1,400 years apart. They are all in agreement about God. They are all in agreement about His story of man, man's diabolical rebellion, and the plague that envelopes the world with Satanic lies.

How is it that so many men (40+), over such a long span of time (1,400+ years), could all be so accurate in their prophetic telling of man's demise and savior? Who or what could have guided their pens in such a perfect manner as to predict the veiled rise of The Prophet? In hindsight, it seems better to ask:

- How could men have overlooked the false prophet and the masquerading light that is being worshiped on the Temple Mount?

- How is it that so many people have studied God's Word over the centuries, yet they rejected the application and how His warnings describe The Prophet and his god?

Those who know Jesus hear His voice. From His Word, they know that another man, a villainous thief, was to appear sometime after His ascension. For the faithful, these events are absolutes. We know that if God is God, then there must be a game-changing prophet; someone who contradicts all the rest. The Bible gives us this man's many names. He is the epitome of evil – a murderous thief who dares to adopt Jesus' place, throne, and titles as his own. The biblical Word is precise in the way it describes the many things this man would say and even offers specific details about the way he would say them. Through the pens of prophets, his character is chronicled ad nauseam. We have been offered the predetermined knowledge of his many atrocious accomplishments and warned about his stunning ability to deceive. Author after author warned us about the man who would oppose God's chosen people and oppress Jesus' followers. Yet men, even some of the elect, refuse to accept the prophetic occurrences that have been fulfilled. Why does the world reject the evidence?

When the fog of delusion is emboldened and anchored by normalcy bias, men rely upon their strongest argument – *denial*. This so-called *ostrich effect* keeps people from seeing what they do not want to see. This very real human tendency infects and affects even some of God's most trusting followers.

Nonetheless, we have been warned about a man known and characterized as *the antichrist*, who will appear and convince many that God has no son. It seems reasonable to assume that any supposed 'prophet of God' who appeared after Christ and boastfully proclaimed that "God has no son" would immediately be recognized as *the* antichrist or, at the very least, *an* antichrist. So, when such a man appeared and said, *"The Beneficent (God) has no son..."* aren't we in the ballpark? By the very definition of *antichrist*, this man and his members are certainly members of that villainous club!

Still, the world awaits another.

The Word of God teaches us that those who kill in the name of God do not know the Father and His Son. Did you get that? **Those who kill, thinking they are doing a service to God, do not know God.** There are no exceptions. God has not changed His mind and decided that we should pick up the stones that Jesus taught us to drop. But history has offered up a self-proclaimed prophet of God, a belligerent antichrist, who has convinced many that killing in the name of God is the highest form of worship. He went a step further and convinced billions of people that killing in the name of God is a requirement that gains them passage into paradise. In other words, he taught people that they can earn their way to God through murder.

Still, the world awaits another.

We've been taught that a physical image of the liar, the son of the dawn, will acquire Jesus' title as *the bright Morning Star*. We know this simply because God would not use this term to mock His own Son. God would not mock His gift to mankind – the selfless sacrifice of His own Son. God would not mock Jesus' role as *the lamp of light* in the temple of God. God would not mock that which pleases Him. The evident mockery of Lucifer, whose name is found only in the King James Version of Isaiah 14, is directed exclusively at the man who has made kingdoms tremble for 14 centuries. This cause of trembling was the speaking image of the god called *The Dawn*. This same image, the man, expressed that he was the foremost to serve God as God's metaphorical son. Hence, he is literally known as the *son of the Dawn*. What a strange coincidence this is! His recorded testimony boasts of him being *the bright morning star* as well as *the son of the dawn*. The reader might want to compare this to the mockery given in Isaiah 14:12. Imagine that! Lucifer denied that Jesus Christ was the Son of God and then assumed the role of the son of God as a metaphorical reference to himself. In so doing, he claimed the throne that belongs to Jesus. What an arrogant fool!

Calling himself *the star of piercing brightness that appears at the end of the night*, this notorious antichrist prophet attempted to unseat the Messiah. Because *the bright Morning Star* is Jesus' title in John's book of Revelation, Isaiah's biblical warning makes a few of the faithful understandably uncomfortable. But now the reader knows the difference between the two in that the one being mocked by God is the liar, the metaphorical son of the dawn who attempted to steal what rightfully belongs to the Son of God.

Still, the world awaits another.

We've been warned that a man with eyes and a boastful mouth will call himself *The Most High*. Such a man has appeared and was recorded saying, "... I am the foremost to serve God." It's hard to imagine any man placing himself above the likes of Abraham, Moses, David, Isaiah, Daniel, John, Paul, and the rest of God's prophets. But to place oneself above the Son of God... that's simply Luciferian!

Still, the world awaits another.

We've been warned about the false prophet. The Word tells us that he will oppose Jesus' teaching and he will attempt to change the Laws of the Father. These are the same Laws that have been in place and recognized by Jews and Christians since their inception 3,300 ago. Of course, Christians adopted these Jewish Laws in the years following Jesus' appearance, crucifixion, and resurrection. As we all know, Jesus is a perfectly lawful Jew. He is specific in telling us that He did not come to change the Law but to fulfill it! However, Jesus' opposer had other ideas. He changed the Laws. He changed the Laws, declaring that the changes were improvements over Laws that were long-since outdated. No prophet of God changed any of God's Laws – never! Instead, Jesus' saving grace changed the outcome of condemnation from His Father's Laws. The men who dropped their stones of righteous judgment did not hear Jesus tell them that the prostitute did nothing wrong. She was a prostitute who was caught in the act of fornication! According to God's Laws, she had earned and deserved death. Death is the wage of sin. However, Jesus caused those 'righteous men' to recognize that their hands were not clean – they were not righteous. Like the prostitute, each one of them had done something in their past to earn the same wage as the woman. They, too, had earned death. The only thing that stood in the way of the prostitutes' earned wage was the gift of the Son. He stands in the way of that earned wage for you and me still today.

The false prophet, however, chose to re-introduce 'righteous judgment' and execute it with his own hands. The laws and the rules surrounding this righteous judgment were something of his own determination. Many of his scholars, those who have studied this man's teaching and who narrate his speech, go so far as to say of him...

"... the law of [The Prophet] is decidedly superior to and more comprehensive than the previous laws..."

This is just a slight part of the documented evidence concerning the man who chose to change God's Laws. Daniel warned us about him. Paul, the Comforter, warned us about him. Yet billions of people teach as this man taught. This lone man, he who Daniel described as *the little horn*, had eyes, a boastful mouth, a desire to change the Laws, and the audacity to place himself above the Son of the Living God. And it doesn't end there!

Still, the world awaits another.

We've been warned about a man who will appear and be recognized by three numeric symbols. Most understand these symbols to be the numbers 666. This has stumped people for nearly 2,000 years. As it turns out, the number system that translates into 666 is a Western Arabic system that was developed a thousand years after the original biblical warning was penned. Here's the rub... The original symbols were Greek numerals that were not intended to be translated. The number does not matter. What matters is the symbolic nature, the image, of the Greek numerals themselves. When utilized as puzzle pieces, these three Greek symbols make up The Prophet's calligraphic name. It is that simple. As a collective body, we have all been stumped over this overly simple, three-piece child's puzzle. It has been puzzling for one reason and one reason alone, this was not to be seen until *the proper time*. Seeing his name now, using the three original Greek numerals, we can rest assured that the man who called himself *the Most High* is the man named in Revelation 13:18. His is the name that has baffled us for centuries. What are the odds that the antichrist prophet who changed God's Laws just so happens to make his name out of the same symbols written into Revelation? From this day forward, people will know him to be *the beast out of the earth!* Can these things be merely coincidental? Those who understand mathematical probability would have to say no.

Still, the world awaits another.

We've been warned that a very bad actor will appear upon this earth in a bid to oppose God's chosen people and oppress Jesus' followers. Originally, this opposition and oppression was instituted by The Prophet's own hand and actions. It is currently carried on by his ever-growing, militaristic band of Prophetiers. It has already been established that he and his army have attempted to change the Laws of God to something more fitting to him and his god. Now, his new standard of time can be addressed. By his direction, his body of believers has set up a new calendar. This new calendar honors his journey and rise to prophethood. They see the year as 1441 A.H. His followers use the world standard, Anno Domini, or A.D. (the year of our Lord), as a secondary measure of time.

Still, *the world awaits another.*

We've been warned that Lucifer, a man, will be mocked in his death. Careful reading of the chapter reveals that he is not mocked for making kingdoms tremble. Yet, he has made them tremble. He is not mocked for overthrowing its cities and making the world a desert. Yet, he has overthrown its cities and made the world a desert. He **is** mocked for being nothing more than a man. History knows such a man. It is he who has made kingdoms tremble, overthrown its cities, and, through the Prophetiers, continues in his efforts to make the world a desert. He has accomplished this through deception. He continues to achieve these goals through his own recorded directives and marks - written instructions gathered for those who intend to carry out his father's wishes. These are a people who have been taught to steal, kill, and destroy in the name of God. They do as he did. He missed Jesus' lesson about sinners and the stones they throw. Though the statement about his people stealing, killing, and destroying makes reasonable men cringe, it cannot be factually denied or dismissed as erroneous. These required deeds have not been misunderstood or misinterpreted. The learned actions and deeds of his people are in written form. With the information being offered here and on a global scale, denying the existence of such directives is now merely a form of intentional ignorance. Our politically correct world demands that such statements, factual as they may be, not to be made about any one man or membership. Yet the Word warns us about this very character and the many people he would lead astray. It's happening! When things become even slightly uncomfortable for the false prophet and his sympathizers, our PC culture serves as a great form of defense and a phenomenal ally of their own!

Mocked in his death for being no more than a man, we can reasonably assume that Lucifer has lived and died – just as it has been written. According to prophetic testimony, he had to die prior to his being revealed. Isaiah wrote about his death. Daniel wrote about his death. Among the many things that separate Christ from the antichrist is the nasty business of maggots and worms that accompany burial. Jesus was entombed and lay above ground for three days. Then He was resurrected. But Lucifer was thrown into a grave and covered by blankets of maggots and worms – for eternity. Unfortunately, his vile intrigue continues. His deceit has carried far beyond the grave. Though he has long-since been dead, his power and influence have never been stronger than they are today. His elected officials have been seated in the highest government capacities and they have infiltrated the offices of most nations around the world. His changed laws are being implemented globally, primarily by lethal force. His ever-growing voting blocks are becoming the norm and they push a deceptive narrative of peace and morality. What his followers conveniently leave out of their declarations is that this supposed *peace* comes only when all nations and religions bow a knee to his god. His living army is nearly two billion strong and their numbers nearly double when accounting for their political allies. With the Prophetiers continually growing and our culture shifting more and more toward political correctness, this man and his body have attained the unthinkable. It is as John asks, "Who can make war against the beast?"

Still, the *world awaits another.*

We've been warned that Lucifer will attempt to replace the Messiah and say:

- I will ascend to heaven
- I will raise my throne above the stars of God
- I will sit enthroned on the mount of assembly
- I will make myself like the most high

What a boastful mouth this man has! The stunning thing about these statements and his mouth is that the world already knows him. He's described as a prophet of God who rejects God as our Father. He rejects the Son. He's The Prophet who declared that he ascended to heaven early in his prophethood. He's the man who placed himself above all his predecessors and said he is the foremost to serve God. He is the man who said he was to be raised to perfection and proclaimed that he was to become like The Most High.

Still, the world *awaits another.*

We've been warned that an intriguing character, one who secretly plans something illicit, will appear upon the face of the earth. The Word is that he will oppose the teaching of Jesus. We are told that he will become very powerful and most stern. We are told that he will cause astounding devastation and succeed in whatever he does. We are warned that he will destroy the mighty men and the holy people. We are told that he will cause deceit to prosper and that he will consider himself superior. The world knows a man who has accomplished all these things.

Two of Jesus' disciples were corrected for arguing over which one was closest and most loved by Jesus. Though the body of the harlot will protest, faithful Christians understand that no such position exists. There is no prophet in the first position. However, The Prophet leapfrogs all of that and declares that he is the most high. According to him, Jesus is not the Son of God, and He did not die on the cross. Apparently, things like truth, evidence, witnesses, Old Testament prophecies, and all the Apostles were mistaken! Yet they described Jesus and His opposition perfectly!

We are told that this terrifying man will destroy many by peace. We are told that he will oppose the Truth by killing in the name of God. He has led a global nation that acts in such a manner. The world witnessed this man's 'peace' on February 26, 1993 and again on September 11, 2001. We witnessed his version of 'peace' on September 11, 2012; April 15, 2013, and again on December 2, 2015. We watched as his 'peace' was demonstrated November 26-29, 2008, January 7, 2015, and November 18, 2015. Like it or not, the world is acquainted with him and his tactics. Being the ostriches that most people are, they refuse see what their eyes have captured. They refuse to hear what their ears have heard. Over fear of reprisal, most refuse to challenge his institution of peace, making him everything we were warned he would be.

Still, the world awaits *another.*

We've been warned that Lucifer would raise himself above all others, like some sort of king. We've been warned that he would show no regard for the gods of his fathers. Instead, he would introduce a new god, one with new rules and new laws. Lucifer would introduce a foreign god who masquerades as God and attempt to steal God's glory.

We've been warned that he will honor this new god with gold and silver, with precious stones and costly gifts. Such a man has come about! He honors his god with a teaching he calls *GOLD*. His golden temple is unmistakable in its many photographs and brochures. It is abominable in meaning. Seen standing where it does not belong, that gold dome now occupies a desolate ground – void of any prayers to God.

He honors his god with silver - namely a silver signet ring. He used this ring to seal letters that he was not capable of writing himself. As the world should know he was illiterate – incapable of reading or writing anything on his own.

He honors his god with precious stones; three blackened and broken pieces of rock that are currently held together by a ring of silver. They adorn an exterior corner of this man's principal house of worship. Lucifer calls these gathered pieces of precious stone *the cornerstone*. He claims that these stones combine to make up the biblical *cornerstone*. Again, he denies Jesus in this role as the Rock that the founders rejected. One can't help but notice that these broken pieces of stone come with a biblical parallel with the house of Baal. He and The Prophet share a similar fondness for this unremarkable rock. Baal's account of the sacred stone can be found in 2 Kings 10:26-27. With the precious cornerstone broken and burned, it readily describes the stone that was removed from the house of Baal. And the irony continues! The Prophet has openly acknowledged that his house of worship was used as a latrine during the time of his prophethood. Knowing that the house of Baal would ultimately be utilized as a latrine, the stories about these two houses seem to be one and the same. The reader might ask what came first, the history or the prophecy? Since the similarities between the two have not been recognized until now, it is reasonable to conclude that history and prophecy seem to have met in this time. Of course, it could be just another coincidence. But how many coincidences does it take before the world recognizes that none of this is coincidence?

Lastly, this exalted king honors his god with the highest priced gifts of all - the lives and souls of men. He justifies his acts of murder as actions consistent with *Voluntary Gifts* to his god. In effect, he sacrifices people to his god.

Still, the world awaits another.

We've been warned that Jesus' nemesis would be a thief. This is a literal reference. As a *righteous* thief, this guy taught others to steal on behalf of him and on behalf of the god he introduced. Can it be just another coincidence that the man spoken of here, this literal thief, boasted about his ongoing career of pillaging while simultaneously declaring himself to be a prophet of God? Is it coincidence that this man acted in a manner consistent with Jesus' warning in John 10:10? The consistency of The Prophet's actions mirroring biblical warning is nothing less than fascinating! His body of believers, billions of them, admire and worship him for these actions. They consider him to be the perfect model for men!

Still, the world awaits another!
We've been warned about a thief who comes in the night. Most of us get the image of a man breaking into a house under the cover of darkness. But the biblical warning, God's description of the false prophet, is given with specific intent. The boastful thief has convinced billions of Christ deniers that he is *the bright morning star* - the light that comes at the end of darkness. Though death tied his tongue centuries ago, he continues to speak through that misleading little book. Remember Isaiah's warning; "Woe to those who call evil good and good evil, who put darkness for light and light for darkness, who put bitter for sweet and sweet for bitter"? All of these are references to the false prophet, his foreign god, and the little book they have presented. No longer does man have to ponder the curious statement Jesus made about 'coming like a thief in the night.' Just as the light that breaks on a new day is called the dawn, both men have made the claim. Each declares that he is the light known as *the bright Morning Star*. But only one of these men has the benefit of God's many prophets describing Him as the star and the light. Written testimony was given long before Jesus' arrival. This testimony has been verified by those who learned from Jesus. Many of them accompanied Him when He walked the earth as a man. And we have the testimony of Paul, he who learned from Jesus *after* Jesus' crucifixion and ascension. Paul is the living vessel of the Spirited *Comforter* that Jesus speaks of. It is of little wonder why The Prophet rejects Paul's testimony and steals the title of *Comforter* as his own. In accordance with the work of Satan (the masquerading light), the false prophet also masquerades as a form of light. Specifically, he speaks of himself as the *light-giving lamp* - a reflection of the light that is his god. He made this declaration on his own account. The evidence is in. The proof has been delivered. Our world is soon to learn that only one of these two men is proven to be the Lord as the bright Morning Star. The other is proven to be the liar Lucifer - the man who made kingdoms tremble.

STILL, the world awaits another!
We've been warned about a beast, a vile and despicable man, who will appear upon the face of the earth and masquerade as God's speaking image. Like the Lamb, he would

be flesh and spirit. But, unlike the Lamb, the beast speaks not the truth of God, but the deceptive lies of the dragon he represents. Declaring himself to be *the seal of the prophets*, he contradicts previous biblical testimony and claims to correct the wrongs of the prophets before him – all of them. We are speaking of God's prophets - men like Moses, Isaiah, Jeremiah, Daniel, Matthew, Mark, and Luke. We are referring to the men who spoke and wrote the Word of God. The written Word began with Moses sometime near 1,300 B.C. and was completed by Paul and John in approximately 100 A.D. These are the men who provided God's testimony – all of it. Though the Romans will likely protest, God's written Word ended with Paul and John. There are no viable traditions or rules that contradict previous testimony. Five hundred years after these last two authors set aside their pens, along comes the beast out of the earth – Satan's speaking image.

    While verbally attacking and attempting to negate the written Word, The Prophet exercised all the authority of the original liar. He contradicted and opposed the written testimony of those who came before him. With a blood-drenched sword, he forced the earth and its inhabitants to worship the dragon as *The Light*. He claimed that his revelations were miraculous and that the recorded testimony he gave bears his *mark*. These marks, his spoken and recorded word, have created the image of the god he testifies for. His verbal testimony gave literal breath to the image of the beast that empowered him. His verbal account was that breath. That image was captured in a book. All he had to do was speak the marks that echoed in his mind. When collected as a whole, these marks became the man known as Lucifer and created the image of the beast known as the dragon. Because of his being illiterate, the speaking image knew and understood the Word of God and the prophets as it was verbalized by other men or by the whisperings of the menace found within his own mind. The evidence has been gathered. Historical and current accounts demonstrate how The Prophet and his Prophetiers force everyone to abide by his marks and obey his laws. He considers man's refusal to abide by his laws to be acts of war. His oppressive scheme became so heavy handed that men and women who lived within his reach could no longer buy or sell without showing evidence of relying upon a *faith balance*. By his rule, buying and selling were permissible only for those who held onto the marks and practiced the faith only he taught. In the free world, the rule about buying and selling does not hold. But look to Afghanistan or travel the highway of the pilgrims as they make their way to the annual gathering. The rule about buying and selling holds fast! Aside from global sales of the desert's blood, the Prophetiers know to submit to the rule of buying and selling. The reader might find it ironic that Lucifer turns the world into a desert and that his Prophetiers sell the only thing that a desert can offer - desert's blood or oil.

STILL, THE world awaits another!

We've been warned about the appearance of the son of perdition, also known as the man of lawlessness. He is the man who will deceive and oppose everything that is called God. He will exalt himself over everything that is worshiped as God. Men know and understand that the speaking image of God, Jesus, is worshiped as God. The Prophet opposes Him. He exalts himself above Jesus. The Prophet calls his god *the Most High* and his book eludes that he will rise to attain that same position. Doesn't that qualify him as making the declaration that he and his god are above the Father and Son – the God that he says doesn't exist? With the image of *The Light* being found in *The Lamp*, can the reader now understand how The Prophet exalted himself over and above God? The Prophet denied the Son. He denied the Father. But the prophets of the Old and New biblical Testaments represent God as a father. In addition to his contradictory testimony, it seems fair to say that The Prophet's denial of the Father and His Son implicates him as opposing everything that is called God. His own actions and documented testimony reveal that he has set himself up in the temple of God as God! But this should be obvious and easy to see – right? No! Most people, including many of God's elect, do not know what it is that makes up the temple of God. It's certainly not the stone temple in Jerusalem. The temple of God is the Lord God Almighty and His Lamb. The Lord God Almighty is the light, and the Lamb is the Lamp of His light. Knowing this, how might our nefarious villain, The Prophet, set himself up in the temple of God and declare himself to be God? The answer is simple! He claims that his god is the light and that he is the lamp of that light. With his marks, he has set himself up in God's temple, declaring himself to be God as the lamp of light. Remember how God mocks Lucifer for masquerading as the morning star? Well, he masquerades as the lamp of light as well. He has discarded everything that is called God and assumed the role as his own. What could be any more of an abomination than a false prophet and fake god stealing the glory of God as the light and its lamp? What is that abomination that adorns the Temple Mount today? What is that honorary golden dome that has risen from the dust of the Jewish Temples in Jerusalem? What prophet and god does that dome of gold glorify? The significance of reality greatly outweighs the inconvenience of fear this is certain to cause. It matters not if the temple of God that John writes about is spiritual or physical, The Prophet has set himself up in both places. He has assumed Jesus' role in the temple of God as God.

STILL, THE WORLD awaits another!

We've been taught that Jesus saw Satan fall like *lightning* from heaven to earth. John describes Satan as a *blazing star* that fell upon the waters – poisoning them. Previously, it was discussed how this blazing star fell like lightning which makes the sound of thunder. So, when a powerful angel comes down from heaven, described as the sun, blazing like a star, and roaring like thunder - who might this angel be? Is it reasonable to consider that he is the powerful and fallen angel Satan? He is described as holding a little book. Lightning, the blazing star, holds a little book in his right hand and we can hear the roar of its seven thunders. Just what might these seven sounds of lightning be saying? What seven statements are so blasphemous that they have earned biblical mention without the honor of quotation? Might they be the seven summarizing statements of the little book that lays open in the fallen angel's hand? And what book might this be? What book is the image of Satan (as the lightning) and contains seven verses so *oft-repeated* that they create a roar when spoken by the Prophetiers on bended knees?

And where does all of this take place? John says that the blazing star stands with one foot on the sea and one foot on the land. Isn't that a description of the seashore? That is where Satan stands. Look to Revelation 13:1. Look to both - the KJV and the NIV Bibles. In a prophetic vision, the seashore is where John and Satan are standing together. This is the place where John takes the little book out of Satan's hand and eats it. Mistaken for honey, the words of that little book quickly turn bitter in the stomach of a true prophet of God. This bitter turn of biblical testimony explains why John was forbidden to write down the lightning's seven thunders. They are not trustworthy nor are they true. They do not qualify as the sweet honey of God's Word. They are the bitter lies of the fallen angel.

Who else warned us about Satan's deceptive covenant and the voice of his seven bitter statements? Who else warned us about the *one seven* but did not write them down? It was Daniel who warned us about Satan's covenant. It was Daniel who warned us about the seven barks of the lightning's thunder. It was Daniel who warned us about the abomination that stands on a wing of the temple in Jerusalem. Is it just another coincidence that The Prophet's recorded testimony begins with just seven verses? Is it just coincidence that these seven verses are intended to honor the most high god and that they were introduced by his speaking image? And what about that 4th verse, the verse in the middle of the seven? What is so special about the middle verse that it gets special recognition? The answer is that it puts an end to the sacrifice and offering of God. Because of their dedication to The Prophet and his god, the Prophetiers do not benefit from the sacrifice and offering - the gift of God. Instead, they rely upon the lightning for help. They reject God's chosen people and dismiss His gift. The 7th thunder calls out God's chosen people and Jesus' faithful as those who are on the wrong path. And how can it be coincidental that the word *honey* is used as a description of the *marks* found within the little book that's held in the fallen angel's hand?

More and more coincidences. But they are not coincidences at all! It is time. It is time for Jesus' body to see the *abomination that causes desolation* standing before us. It is time to see the masquerading light and his masquerading lamp. It is time to recognize that these things stand where they do not belong. It is time for the end that is decreed to be poured out on the blazing star and the abominations he has set up. From the mouth of one man was delivered the rebellion that created all of this.

STILL, THE WORLD AWAITS another!

We've been taught that Jesus will not return, and His body of Christians will not be captured up *until* the false prophet's rebellion occurs *and* the man of lawlessness is revealed. Why is there so much confusion about this? According to Paul, there is only *one thing* holding back Jesus' return and our being gathered to Him. We wait *only* for the liar to be revealed. The world awaits the unveiling of the man of lawlessness. He's the biblical liar. He's the false prophet. He's the son of a masquerading dawn. He's the son of the original evil. His identity and grand rebellion must be unveiled. We await only his unveiling. His masquerade is all that holds Jesus back.

Such a man has slipped into history. He has made his mark among men. His opposition to Jesus, the preincarnate *Prince of princes*, is well documented. His desire to unseat the Christ and assume His Throne is evident. Jesus, the Word of God, is clear about the differences between Himself as the bright Morning Star and the thief who tells the world that he's the bright morning star. Jesus, the Lamp and sacrificial Lamb, came about to give us life and give us life to the full. But the thief came to do what thieves do. Murder and theft are their trades. History now tells us which of these two men is the Lord and which is the liar.

STILL, THE WORLD AWAITS ANOTHER!

The fog of delusion is dense and long-lasting. But the many traditional scenarios causing men to look past the evidence and wait for another biblical villain are splintering under the mountainous weight of prophetic realities. This man's kingdom has reached a breaking point. The fog is lifting. The confusing babel demonstrated by multiple languages has been set aside and dissipated. Narration of the little book by one of The Prophet's own scholars eliminates the tedious arguments of wrongful or false interpretations. Men can now rely upon the recorded testimonies and valid histories of these two morning stars and come to a few reasonable conclusions:

- By revealing The Prophet, we can verify that one man was the false prophet, little horn, man of lawlessness, stern-faced king, king who exalted himself, beast out of the earth and antichrist
- By revealing The Prophet, we have proof of God
- By revealing The Prophet, God has been validated
- By revealing The Prophet, the God of Israel is Father, Son, and Spirit
- By revealing The Prophet, we have the truth in His Word
- Truth in His Word was delivered by His two Witness
- The two witnesses are His Son and His Spirit - the three agree on all things
- In agreement, they warn about the speaking image of the masquerading light
- The speaking image is *Lucifer* and the masquerading light is *Satan*
- Their attempt to change the laws are evidence of their rebellion
- By revealing The Prophet, nothing remains to inhibit Jesus' return

The Word warns us about the speaking image of the dragon, the man who speaks on behalf of the devil, and the rebellion they would advance upon this earth. The intent is to deceive. Satan and his sidekick of flesh do not agree with the Father and His Two Witnesses. Though there have been many false prophets since Jesus walked the earth, there has been only one who has succeeded in every biblical account of his coming. We see The Prophet in all that he has done, not in all that he is to do. It is finished. He has created a lawless and destructive body who does not know the Father and His Son. His murderous rendition of *peace* is the rebellion that has come about men like a plague. The son of perdition is made known, revealed by the truth of the Word. God is not a prankster. There is no *psych* moment or punchline to be found here. The biblical menace has a name. How could there be another? There is no biblical argument that supports two men who are to fulfill these prophecies. There is only The Prophet and the harlot who courts him. She has fulfilled her own biblical warnings. The two are often confused as one but now they are easily distinguished as the king and queen of a revived Babylon. The king has accomplished all that is written about him and his rebellion. The harlot and the world's *P.C. Elite* have made their alliances with him. Via documented testimony, the Word of God has now been proven perfect in the historical revelation of the biblical bad. Most in this kingdom will scoff at the evidence. They will gnash their teeth and growl with threats of attack. They will point their fingers and scream accusations of bigotry and hatred. This, too, is biblically prophetic.

Don't fall asleep. Don't get drunk on the maddening wine of Babylonians – the filth of abomination poured from a golden Babylonian cup. Don't be swayed by the loudspeakers or detoured by the sound of the seven thunders as they deliver the lies of the speaking image in his native language. Don't be lulled into a false sense of reason or be blinded by the delusion that the world will accept that The Prophet is and was the worst model of humanity. Remember, this world belongs to him and his god. This is his kingdom. This is their eternal home. No amount of evidence, historical or written, will open the eyes and ears of the hopelessly deluded. They refuse to love the truth because they delight in wickedness. Keep in mind that the false prophet has only to be revealed for Jesus to return and collect His body. The world does not have to be convinced of Lucifer's historical identity before the elect go home. After all, our world cannot understand or accept simple truths. No longer do men recognize that *illegal* means *lawless*. No longer do men accept that being born with a penis defines a man as *male*. And, somewhere along the way, men changed God's definition of *marriage* from that of a man and a woman, together *becoming one* flesh, to that of a man becoming one with whatever soothes his depraved mind. What is clearly written as *detestable* to God has become the definition of *love* in this wicked and rebellious world. This is a surprise only to men. God warned of this falling away long ago.

Forget about convincing the majority that the false prophet has set his disciples among our ranks. It was the majority who welcomed their placement! We now live in a world where sweet has become bitter. For many, the marks of Lucifer have become the new words of God. But God has no new words. Nothing has changed. We now live in a world where darkness has become light – with the masquerading light worshiped as God. We now live in a world where evil has become good – with the thief becoming the model of perfection.

Revealing the man of lawlessness is one thing. Convincing others about his identity is another thing entirely. Our Father has the final say. He will convince the world with His perfect timing and judgment. He gave people 2,000 years to accept His Son's selfless act of sacrifice and offering as a gift and paid ransom. As prophesied, only a few accepted God's Son. For most who deny Him, Jesus' gift of ransom will not stand between the naysayer and the Father's judgment. Among the fallen are those who make up the body of the harlot and the beast she rides. They might call Jesus, *Lord, Lord*, but they refuse to obey His commands. She and the beast have become victims of their own traditions and false teachings. Just as those who choose to ignore the obvious biological aspects that separate a man from a woman, this generation of man largely chooses to ignore the tremendous offering of love given by the Father and His Son.

All things considered, matching biblical prophecies about Jesus' nemesis to the historical character who fulfilled them was a journey of loving duty. Albeit daunting at times, God has earned the attention of men. Initially, few wanted to hear it. Even fewer wanted to discuss it. But things have changed. The world has become woefully lawless. This generation is promoting actions and mannerisms that God detests. The wicked rebellions we see today are hidden and protected under a veil of forced obedience falsely known as *tolerance*. This is prophetic. God knew how men would act when He said *all* nations would oppose Jerusalem – *His Jerusalem*. Though difficult to watch, even these United States have turned from a Judeo-Christian nation into something detestable and unrecognizable. The majority now opposes the Father and Son. It has become so vile that one arm of our governing body was recently recorded *booing* the name of God while championing infanticide and detestable relationships.

Christian children are taught to follow Jesus and love our neighbors as we love ourselves - while cautioned not to approve of detestable acts. For these beliefs, Christians are deemed to be *hateful* by our public schools and officials. To get along, they must hide their morality and faith in God from the authorities who teach and govern public education. This should come as a surprise to no one. God has not been welcomed in our school system for decades. God's Word and our Christian children's obedient behavior are now cause for being outcast.

Becoming a historic reality in life and death, the false prophet had to be revealed by name. From this day forward, he will be. Thus, Jesus has been proven to be the Messiah. Even science agrees. By way of mathematics and the science of probability, Peter W. Stoner & Robert C. Newman (Science Speaks) proved that Jesus is the Messiah of prophecy. The false prophet has been proven in similar fashion. It can be nothing other. Mathematically speaking, it's impossible for there to be another man who will match all these prophetic warnings. Again, God is not trying to catch us in a *gotcha* moment. He wants His elect to recognize Jesus and His opposition. That is why He was so explicit in His many descriptions.

Gathering the evidence about the false prophet was accomplished by comparing three books and reviewing 1,400 years of history. This book is meant to be used as a summary that assists the reader in matching the many biblical warnings with the written and historical accounts of the man who fulfilled them. The sad reality is that a politically correct world serves deceit well. Because of the highly charged political environment in which we now live, his very recognizable name is not mentioned in the body of this book. His followers are not mentioned by their religious affiliation. They are not addressed by the name he gave them. His political allies are not mentioned by name. They are all mentioned by character. Like rabid dogs, his body of believers and political allies will fight against the evidence offered here. They will do so with accusations of hatred, bigotry, and intolerance. They will accuse – just like the father of lies accused his brethren. In this kingdom, truth has yielded to narrative. The world cares little about the difference between fact and fiction. It cares only about how we make people feel. But facts are facts, and the world cannot change the facts. Verifiable facts are offered within this book. No man or body can change the things The Prophet said or the things he did. They cannot change history. Hatred is defined by those who ignore Jesus' demonstration of love through grace. Jesus stood between the prostitute and those who thought they were righteous enough to institute God's judgment with stones, delivered by their own, sinful, hands. What is it that God says about the Accuser? "The Accuser has been hurled down… the devil has gone down to you! He is filled with fury because he knows that his time is short." So, the accusations will come.

Hatred opposes love. Love knows and reflects grace. Grace is a characteristic that The Prophet lacks. His hatred is well demonstrated by those who murder by his command. This, they say, is a part of their religious duty. But stealing, killing, and destroying oppose God's Ten Commandments and are readily determined to be sinful. To perform these acts in God's name is simply blasphemous and founded in hate. God said, "Those who hate me love death." But the liar has altered the sentiment. According to The Prophet: "Those who wage war against [him] and [his god], and who commit mischief [by opposing their newfound laws] in the land, shall be *murdered* or *crucified*…" There has been no nullification or alteration to this command. When confronted with this, the Prophetiers might cry *mis-interpretation* or *metaphorical*, but their actions exude submission. The liar has changed murder from a sinful act into a dutiful endeavor. Evil has become good. God does not contradict His own Words - He fulfills that which was previously spoken. Those who kill thinking they are doing a service to God do not know God. This accounts for the horrific actions of the Prophetiers. Hate opposes love just as murder opposes God.

Bigotry is defined as "intolerance toward those who hold different opinions from oneself." The proclamation that faithful Christians are *bigots* has become vogue and a necessity for the lawless in this ever-progressive kingdom. Christians have been and always will be among the minority. This is nothing new. What's new is the hatred found in the hearts of the street urchins who gnash their teeth and foam at the mouth when demanding the acceptance and approval of the new state of Sodom. What's new is the identity of the harlot who has been calling faithful Christians *bigots* for over 17 centuries now. Yet, truth is truth. The accusation of bigotry, in this sense, is little more than a weapon of offense. Every man is entitled to his own opinion. But no man is entitled to his own facts. The Prophet might have benefitted from knowing the difference.

Intolerance is defined as "unwillingness to accept views, beliefs, or behaviors that differ from one's own." The accusation has become another weapon that is used as an arrow to maim or kill any argument or suggestion that the Prophetiers submit to the bitter words of the worst of mankind. This arrow can be found in the quiver of all who oppose the Word of God. It is by this definition that the loving Son of God, He who gave His life for us, has been found intolerant. His love, truth, and grace have been rejected as intolerant in the new Sodom. That which God calls *detestable*, this kingdom calls *love*. That which God calls *sinful*, The Prophet calls *dutiful*. The sweet Word of God has become the bitter word of the godless. By the rebellious desires of men, darkness has become light. But the Word remains the same and the un-yielding question holds fast; should God's elect be threatened and bullied into approving the detestable acts of Sodom? Here's the answer... "Although they know God's righteous decree that those who do such things *deserve death*, they not only continue to do these very things but also approve of those who practice them." How can we not grieve for this generation? How can we not grieve for the children who are destined for public education and their immersion into the bitterness of the new word and teaching? Reading, writing and arithmetic have given way to accepting Bruce as Caitlyn, recognizing terror as something godly, and the only thing that now matters is the color of a man's skin. The new objective goals are self-loathing of one's whiteness, participating in female oppression, and celebrating non-binary Birth Certificates. It's as though God was speaking directly to our public educators when He warned about approving of those who reject His righteous decrees. But, in the moment, He was speaking directly to the Romans. The Romans lost their way. Our educators have lost their way. Though few are listening, most can feel the earth begin to shake.

Was The Prophet's planned rebellion a movement of tolerance? What selfless act of sacrifice and offering can be found in his pillaging, plundering, and looting? Has peace been implemented by his never-ending war? Instead of promising to *NEVER FORGET* about the events of September 11, 2001 - maybe the world should soften the expectation to something a little more palatable like "Some people did something…" Of course, that's already been done. The world apologizes for the truth and rejects the law while it bathes in lies and delights in the horrors of the lawless. This willful ignorance has delivered its just fruits in Portland, Seattle, Wuhan, Chicago, New York, Kabul, San Francisco, L.A., Beijing, Kenosha, Tehran, Minneapolis, Damascus, and countless other cities. To those who govern these cities, consider Isaiah's prophetic warning: "Woe to those who call evil good and good evil, who put darkness for light and light for darkness, who put bitter for sweet and sweet for bitter." To those who seek the true story of man, consider what you have learned here. Consider the Word of God, which is compared to the sweetness of honey. Compare it to the Opposer's word - that which he calls *the beverage of many hues that is formed by the bee (honey)*. That word turned bitter in the stomach of a true prophet of God. What appeared to be godly was found wanting, and the supposed *healing for men* made John sick. Woe to those who put bitter for sweet and sweet for bitter!

Consider the Word of God, which plainly warns: Those who kill in the name of God do not know God. Then, compare God's Word of warning to The Prophet's word - teaching men to kill in the name of god. Contrary to The Prophet's teaching, the only thing that lies beneath the shadow of the swords are maggots and worms. Evil remains evil and good remains good. Never does evil become good. This truth has been delivered through the breath of Jesus' mouth. This is His sword. Truth is a witness and it speaks for itself. The truth, historical accounts, and recorded testimony has identified the man of lawlessness for who he has always been – a fraud. Ironically, the truth about the existence of the liar now serves as proof that God exists as Father and Son. Such truths cannot be found within the heart, mind, or mouth of the speaking image of the dragon, but they can be found in the prophecies about his appearance and actions. The Son and the Spirit offered their testimony about The Prophet long before he appeared. With a politically correct world bringing about the final spiral of detestable behavior, Lucifer and the god he introduced are soon to meet their promised end. Thrown from heaven to earth, the pair is never to escape its bonds. They'll never return to heaven above. Their reign of deceit and terror has reached its ultimate end. Though they will rage a final battle, their well-earned eternal torment is soon to descend upon the foreign god and his lone prophet.

The world is soon to learn that the number of his name is...

[Given in the Book]
Amen!

For more information contact the publisher at info@advbooks.com

To purchase additional copies of these books, visit our bookstore at:
www.advbookstore.com

Orlando, Florida, USA
"we bring dreams to life"™
www.advbookstore.com

www.ingramcontent.com/pod-product-compliance
Lightning Source LLC
Chambersburg PA
CBHW070631050426
42450CB00011B/3163